D0061304

FUNDAMENTALS OF MUSIC

A Program for Self-instruction

FUNDAMENTALS OF MUSIC

A Program for Self-instruction

ROBERT A. BARNES
The Ohio State University

McGRAW-HILL BOOK COMPANY
New York   San Francisco   Toronto   London

FUNDAMENTALS OF MUSIC:

A Program for Self-instruction

Copyright © 1964 by McGraw-Hill, Inc. All Rights Reserved. Printed in the United States of America. This book, or parts thereof, may not be reproduced in any form without permission of the publishers. *Library of Congress Catalog Card Number* 64-18895

910111213 HDMB 76543210

MT
6
.B243
F8

FOREWORD

The concept of programmed instruction, which has begun to permeate American education at all levels, is not new, but rather a precise organization of some of the best approaches to learning that successful teachers have used for many years. What is both new and highly encouraging is the increasing desire on the part of some music educators, as well as teachers in other fields, to reexamine methods and materials in terms of primary objectives. The application of programmed instruction to the teaching of music is a step both logical and productive, which is among those factors helping to form some exciting new directions for music education in this country.

BALLOU LIBRARY
BUENA VISTA COLLEGE
STORM LAKE, IOWA 50588

In *Fundamentals of Music*, Robert A. Barnes, an experienced musician and teacher, has presented an implementation of the effective techniques of programmed instruction for the teaching of basic information on music fundamentals. Its content includes elemental information on rhythm, the keyboard, major and minor keys, intervals, and syllables. Upon completing the book, a student with no previous formal experience in music will be able to answer the kinds of questions that appear as "criterion questions" at the beginning of each chapter. I have had the pleasure of examining the thorough documentation that has been gathered by Dr. Barnes to support the effectiveness of this text in producing efficient learning in these basic informational materials. One of the most satisfying results obtained thus far through use of this program of instruction is that every student who has completed it carefully has been able to demonstrate, through tests, a high level of comprehension of the content. Average class scores have fallen between 90 and 100 per cent, with the ranges of scores falling within or close to these limits.

Specifically, this book can be helpful in two ways: (1) it will inform each student regarding his present command of the information contained herein; (2) it will teach thoroughly those areas in which the student is not competent. It is not assumed that the book will in any way serve as a substitute for the teacher in the classroom, but rather that it will be used as an effective aid to both the teacher and the student as they engage in the teaching-learning process. Likewise, no assumption has been made that the book will teach the art of music; instead it provides basic information about music.

Various sections of the text could be assigned as ancillary learning experiences in conjunction with a music fundamentals course, or since only a few hours are normally required for completing the program, a teacher may wish to have the students complete it during the first week. In the latter instance, the obvious advantage is that the book will permit the teacher at the outset of the course to take for granted a specific level of competence on the part of each student in the class.

While this programmed text was designed originally by Dr. Barnes to alleviate some of the problems prevalent in the music education of prospective elementary classroom teachers, I believe that it may find considerable use beyond the limits of that curriculum.

William B. McBride
Professor of Music
The Ohio State University

PREFACE

Those whose responsibility it is to guide prospective elementary classroom teachers as they fulfill the music requirements of their college curriculum frequently face two important problems: (1) the differences in musical background among students are often so extreme that it is difficult to determine for a class an appropriate point at which to begin, and (2) there is seldom sufficient class time allotted to cover adequately the specified content. Sometimes these difficulties are increased by a class which is too large and with individual students who are well-prepared in one phase of music but ignorant in other important aspects of the subject.

This book, which contains information on music fundamentals and normally takes four to six hours to complete, is designed to alleviate some of these difficulties, which concern both the instructor and the student. While it was originally developed to enhance the music learning of future elementary teachers, it has received increasing acceptance by teachers of general music classes in the junior and senior high school; beginning instrumental students in band, orchestra, and piano; students in remedial music-theory classes in college; and by individuals who wish to engage in a home-study program in music.

A Program for Self-instruction

If you have leafed through the pages of this book, you have probably noticed that it does not have a traditional format. It is a programmed text—a rather recent development in education. Programmed books offer to the student several advantages not offered by conventional textbooks.

Briefly, the content of this book, the fundamentals of music, has been broken down into small, logical steps which lead you slowly, easily, and systematically to a place at which you are able to answer some rather complicated questions about music. This book consists of a series of short statements and questions. You are asked to respond in some way to every pertinent idea presented. At first, some of the questions may appear to be extremely simple. Don't, however, be misled by this. Answer each one as carefully and as accurately as you can. When you have answered the question, you will then learn whether or not your response is correct. This system will help you to learn in several ways:

1. *You will not only learn the material, but you will know that you have learned it.* You can be sure that you are on the right track, because each time you answer you are informed immediately whether your answer is right or wrong.

2. *You will not have a chance to daydream.* Perhaps you have had the experience, while reading a book, of suddenly realizing that you have no idea what the last page was about. Your mind can not wander while reading this book, for you will participate actively in the learning process by frequently writing short answers.

3. *You will not have to spend time reading or studying material you already know.* Unlike other textbooks, you will be asked a criterion question at the beginning of each chapter. If you answer the question correctly, you merely skip to the next chapter.

4. *You may work at your own rate of speed.* In learning through this system, you take as much time as you need—moving slowly in difficult parts and as fast as you like in the easier sections.

Robert A. Barnes

CONTENTS

Instructions for Reading this Book

The first step in using this book is to cover completely the shaded area on the left side of the page using a bookmark, a card, a strip of paper, or the like. Please prepare such a mask now, before reading further on this page.

Music

Now, with the shaded column covered, complete this sentence: The title of this book is *Fundamentals of* _____. Write the word on the line using either pen or pencil. Your next move is to slide your mask downward on the shaded column until you uncover the correct answer which is, of course, "Music."

Answer, word, response
Any of these is correct.

Each time *after* you have written an answer, you should slide your mask downward to find out whether you have written the correct _____.

clue

Sometimes you will be given a *clue* to the correct answer. Watch for words in italics, like the one in the first line. The words in italics will usually give you a _____ to the correct answer.

Andrew Jackson
[If you answered this correctly, you merely go on to the next question. If you wrote a wrong answer (James Madison, for example), you must write the correct answer in this column as was done here.]
Andrew Jackson

Write an answer to every question. If you don't know the answer, guess! If, when you check your answer, you find that you have answered a question incorrectly, you must write the correct answer in the answer column under the answer which is given. For example, complete this sentence: The name of the seventh President of the United States is _____ _____. (Two separate lines indicate that two words are needed in the answer.)

Often when a number is required for the answer, you will see this [number] following the answer line. There are now _____ [number] states in the United States.

50

Sometimes a letter will suggest the answer to you. Here is an example:

When a newborn baby is expected, the parents usually wonder whether it will be a boy or a g_____.

girl

Sometimes you will be given a choice between two answers. For example, you have been instructed to write every answer because the act of writing in answers has been found important to learning. If you read through the book writing in some answers and filling in others mentally, you will only _____ [hinder/help] your progress.

hinder

If you begin to get weary and start to make mistakes, take a short *break* from reading. You should always stand up and walk around a little between chapters and more often if needed. A short b_____ from time to time will help your learning.

break

If you wish to *review* sections which you have already completed, begin at the beginning and read every tenth or twelfth question (covering the answer you have already written with your finger or a piece of paper). It is usually very helpful to r_____ this way, particularly if you have been away from the book for a while.

review

After you have completed the entire program, Chapters 8 and 10 will provide a complete review of everything you have learned in this book. In other words, Chapters 8 and 10 will provide a complete r_____ for the whole program.

review

It is very important that you actually *write* the answer. And be sure to *write* your answer before looking at the answer given in the shaded answer column. Your intentions may be honorable, but looking before you *write* will definitely hinder your learning. It is very important that you actually _____ out each answer.

write

If you write a wrong answer, you must write the _____ answer in the shaded answer column under the answer that is given.

right *or* correct

If you make as many as 10 per cent of your responses incorrectly in any one chapter, it would be wise to repeat that chapter. If you do not repeat it, you may have even greater difficulty with the chapters that follow.

Now you know how to use the book. Turn the page and begin with Chapter 1. Do each of the chapters in the order in which it comes.

Rhythm (Part 1)

Time Signatures; Whole, Half, and Quarter Notes and Rests

This book contains ten chapters which, if you follow instructions carefully, will provide you with a great deal of information about music fundamentals.

The first two chapters deal with information about rhythm. After completing the first chapter, you will be able to answer questions which are similar to those which appear on this page.

If you think you can answer these questions before reading the first chapter, write the answers in the spaces at the right and then check your answers on the next page. If you believe that you cannot answer these questions, just turn the page now.

Criterion Questions

1. The first measure in each example is rhythmically complete. Draw *one note* which would complete the second measure.

(a) _____

(b) _____

(c) _____

2. The first measure in each example is rhythmically complete. Draw *one rest* which would complete the second measure.

(a) _____

(b) _____

Here are the correct answers to the criterion questions on the preceding page:

1.

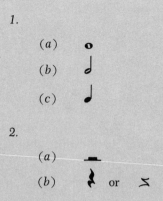

    (a)

    (b)

    (c)

2.

    (a)

    (b)   or

If you missed an answer, or if you do not feel sure of yourself when answering questions of this kind, turn the page and begin with the first frame. Some of the questions may appear to be extremely simple at first, but do not be misled by this.

If you were able to get all five answers right, you may skip to the beginning of Chapter 2.

Regardless of how you answered the questions above, *be sure* you have read "Instructions for Reading this Book" (pages 1–4) before proceeding. Also, do not forget to write the correct answer in the answer column for any question that you answer incorrectly.

notes

high

short

beat

note

o

♩

half

The symbols used on a printed page to represent musical sounds are called *notes*. Here are three different kinds of _____.

o   ♩   ♩

The notes that are printed on the page tell us many things. For one thing, they tell us how *low* or how h_____ the music should sound.

The different kinds of notes tell us a lot about how *long* or how *short* each note should be. By learning the different kinds of notes, we will be able to know just how *long* or how s_____ each note should be sung or played.

Most of our music has a basic pulse or *beat* to which we can march, clap our hands, tap our feet, etc. In knowing how long to hold each note, the b_____ of the music is very important.

As we tap our feet or clap our hands on each beat of the music, one kind of *note* might get several beats while another kind of _____ would receive only one beat.

Here is one kind of note (o). This is called a *whole note*. Draw a whole note. _____

Here is another kind of note (♩). This one is called a *half note*. It is much like the whole note, except that it has a stem on it. Draw a half note. _____

If you know how many beats a whole note (o) is to get in a certain song, you will also know how many beats the half notes should get. The half notes (♩) are always worth just *half* as much as the whole notes. In any piece of music, the half notes are always worth _____ as many beats as the whole notes.

8

If the *whole* notes in a certain song are worth eight beats each, the *half* notes in that song will receive four beats each. Now, suppose the whole notes are worth only four beats; then the half notes would be worth _____ [number] beats. (Just half as much.)

two

How many whole notes do you see here? _____ How many half notes do you see? _____

two

three

𝅝 𝅗𝅥 𝅗𝅥 𝅗𝅥 𝅝

This black note is called a *quarter note* (♩). A quarter note is worth just half as much as the half note. Draw a quarter note. _____

♩

If a whole note (𝅝) is worth eight beats, the half note (𝅗𝅥) will be worth four beats and the quarter note (♩) worth two beats.

Now, if the whole note is worth four beats, the half note will be worth two beats and the quarter note worth _____ [number] beat(s).

one

One whole note is equal in value to two half notes. One whole note is equal in value to _____ [number] quarter note(s).

four

Whole

Half

Quarter

Two quarter notes are equal in value to _____ [number] half note(s). Four quarter notes are equal in value to _____ [number] whole note(s).

one

one

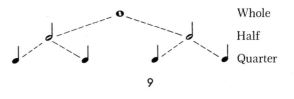

Whole

Half

Quarter

9

This means that these two notes together (♩ ♩) would be equal in value to *one* of another kind of note. Draw this note. _____

Draw a note which has twice the value of the note ♩
_____

Each note here is worth half as much as the one before it. If this whole note is worth eight beats, the half note is worth _____ beat(s) and the quarter note _____ beat(s).

𝅝   𝅗𝅥   ♩
Whole   Half   Quarter

Now, let's do it the other way. If the half note shown is worth two beats, the whole note must be worth _____ beat(s).

𝅝   𝅗𝅥   ♩
Whole   Half   Quarter

If the quarter note shown is worth two beats, the half note must be worth four beats and the whole note _____ beat(s).

Let's assume that this quarter note is worth one beat. The half note is worth _____ beat(s) and the whole note is worth _____ beat(s).

10

In writing music, the notes are placed on a *staff* as shown here. On this staff we see how many half notes? _____ How many quarter notes? _____

two, three

Now, see if you can get this one. This quarter note is worth four beats. The half note is then worth _____ beat(s) and the whole note is worth _____ beat(s).

eight

sixteen

From this, you can see that if we know how many beats any *one* kind of note gets, we can always figure out how many _____ each of the other notes should get.

beats

The $\frac{2}{4}$ on the staff shown below is called a *time signature*. (Sometimes it is called a meter signature.) We use the time _____ in determining what kind of a note is to receive *one* beat.

signature

In order to know what kind of a note is to receive *one beat*, we look at the t_____ signature. Frequently the time signature is only one factor indicating note values and groupings. In most beginning music, however, the time signature provides complete information, and that is the approach taken in this book.

time

11

It is actually the *bottom* number of the time signature that tells us what kind of a note should get *one beat*. In this case, the bottom number is a 4. The number 4 stands for *quarter note*. This time signature tell us that a

quarter

_____ note should receive *one* beat.

It is the *bottom* number of the time signature that tells us what kind of a note is to receive *one* beat. In this case,

bottom

quarter

the _____ number is a 4. So, we know that, in this song, the _____ notes are to receive *one* beat.

In this time signature, the _____ number is a 4, so,

bottom

we know that the quarter note is to receive *one* beat. If the quarter note is worth *one* beat in this song, the half

two

notes will be worth _____ [number] beat(s). (Twice as much as the quarters.)

With this time signature, the _____ notes will

quarter

receive *one* beat each. The *whole* notes will receive

four

_____ [number] beat(s) each.

12

<table>
</table>

2	In this time signature, the bottom number is _____. The number 2 stands for *half note*. In this song the
half	_____ note will receive *one* beat.

half	With this time signature, what kind of note would receive *one* beat? A _____ note.

With this time signature, what kind of note would receive *one* beat? A _____ note.

quarter

The bottom number of the time signature tells us what kind of a note is to receive _____ [number] beat(s). (You will learn of exceptions to this rule in your advanced study of music.)

one

With this time signature, the half notes would receive _____ [number] beat(s) each and the whole notes would receive _____ [number] beat(s) each.

one
two

With this time signature, note *a* would receive _____ beat(s) and note *b* would receive _____ beat(s).

two
one

(*a*) (*b*)

13

two

four

The quarter note would receive one beat.

With this time signature, note *a* would receive _____ beat(s) and note *b* would receive _____ beat(s).

(*a*) (*b*)

note, one beat

The bottom number of the time signature tells us what kind of a _____ receives _____ _____.

measures

The staff is divided by vertical lines called *bar lines*. The spaces between the bar lines are called *measures*. Bar lines on the staff are used to mark off the _____.

measures

On this staff there are four m_____.

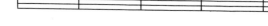

four

Looking carefully at this time signature, we know that there are *four* beats in the first measure, *four* beats in the second measure, and _____ beat(s) in the third measure.

First   Second   Third

three

You found that there were the *same* number of beats in each measure. The *top* number of the time signature tells us how many beats there are in each measure. The *top* number in this time signature tells us that each measure will have _____ beat(s) in it.

The margin answer words:

three
quarter

The *top* number of this time signature tells us that there will be _____ beat(s) in every measure. The *bottom* number tells us that a _____ note will receive *one* beat.

measure
half
one

The *top* number of this time signature tells us that there will be two beats in each _____ of this song. The bottom number tells us that the _____ notes will receive _____ beat(s) each.

note
one beat

The *bottom* number of the time signature (meter signature) tells us what kind of a _____ receives _____ _____. (There are exceptions to this rule, but you will learn of these in your advanced study of music.)

beats, measure

The *top* number of the time signature tells us how many _____ there are in each _____. (There are exceptions to this rule also, which you will learn later in your study of music.)

three

If we *know* that the quarter notes in this song are each worth *one* beat, how many beats are there in each measure? _____

Let's assume that there is a time signature here with a bottom number of 4. This tells us that each quarter note must receive _____ beat(s). The top number tells us the number of beats in *each measure*. The top number in this time signature would have to be _____.

The time signature for this song has a bottom number of 2. What would the *top* number have to be in this time signature? _____

If the bottom number of the time signature for this song was 4, that would mean that each _____ note is worth one beat. If a quarter note is worth one beat, the note at (*a*) is worth _____, the note at (*b*) is worth _____, and the note at (*c*) is worth _____ beat(s).

(*a*)　　(*b*)　　(*c*)

Assuming that the *bottom* number of the time signature is 2, how many beats are in each of these measures? _____ The *top* number of the time signature, then, would have to be _____.

one

2

3

quarter

one

two, four

two

2

Assuming that the bottom number of the time signature is 4, how many beats are in each of these measures? _____ The top number of the time signature, then, would have to be _____.

three

3

If the bottom number of the time signature is 4, what would the *top* number of the time signature be? _____

3

In this time signature, the bottom number is _____. The number 2 stands for *half note*. In this song, the _____ note must receive *one* beat.

2

half

The first measure is complete. Draw a note which would accurately complete the second measure. _____

With this time signature, is this measure complete? _____ [yes/no]

yes

There are four quarter notes which total four beats.

17

no

*The key signa-
ture tells us
that three
beats are
needed. The
two quarter
notes are
worth only one
beat each.*

♩

♩

o

rest

With this time signature, is this measure complete?
_____ [yes/no]

The first measure is complete. Draw *one note* which would accurately complete the second measure. _____

The first measure is complete. Draw *one note* which would accurately complete the second measure. _____

The first two measures are complete. Draw *one note* which will accurately complete the third measure. _____

If a composer wants a silence instead of a sound in his music, he writes a "rest." *Rests* are counted just like notes, and there is a *rest* to correspond to *each* of the different notes. So far, we have talked about three different kinds of notes. There is a _____ to correspond to each of these notes.

The *rest* at (*a*) is a *whole rest*, the rest at (*b*) is a *half rest*, and the rest at (*c*) is a *quarter rest*. If the *whole*

18

rest is worth four beats, the *half* rest will be worth two beats, and the *quarter* rest will be worth _____ beat(s).

one

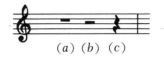

(a) (b) (c)

This is a quarter rest (𝄽). Quarter rests are counted just like quarter notes, so there will be _____ beat(s) in each of these measures.

three

This is a quarter rest (𝄽). Draw a quarter rest. _____

𝄽

If the quarter note is worth one beat, how many beats are in each of these measures? _____

two

With this time signature, is this measure complete? _____ [yes/no]

yes
There are three
  beats:

𝄽 = 1
𝄽 = 1
♩ = 1

This is a half rest. It is placed *on top* of the third line of the staff. Assume that this line is the third line of the staff and draw a half rest on it. _____

19

Draw a *half rest* at number 1 and a *quarter rest* at number 2.

1. ▬

2. 𝄽

1. _____

2. _____

𝄽

The first measure is complete. Draw *one rest* which could be used to complete the second measure. _____

𝄽

Draw a quarter rest. _____

𝄽

A one-beat
  quarter rest is
  needed here.

The first measure is complete. Draw *one rest* which will accurately complete the second measure. _____

no
*There are only
  three beats:*

▬ = 2

𝄽 = 1

With this time signature, is this measure complete? _____ [yes/no]

♩

The first measure is complete. Complete the second measure with *one note*. _____

20

A half rest is needed here.

If you are not too skilled at making quarter rests, just make them the best way you can. You'll improve with practice!

The first measure here is complete. Draw *one rest* which would accurately complete the second measure. _____

The first measure is complete. Draw *one rest* which would accurately complete the second measure. _____

21

Rhythm (Part 2)

*Eighth Notes, Eighth Rests,
Sixteenth Notes, Dotted Notes*

The second chapter gives more information about rhythm. Before proceeding, however, see if you are able to answer the questions below.

If you think you can answer these questions before reading Chapter 2, write the answers in the spaces at the right, and then check your answers on the next page. If you believe that you cannot answer these questions, just turn the page now.

Criterion Questions

1. The first measure in each example is rhythmically complete. Draw *one rest* which would complete the second measure.

(a) ____

(b) ____

2. The first measure in each example is rhythmically complete. Draw *one note* which would complete the second measure.

(a) ____

(b) ____

Here are the correct answers to the criterion questions on the preceding page:

1.

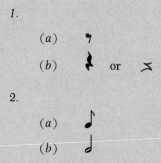

    (a)

    (b)   or

2.

    (a)

    (b)

If you missed an answer, or if you do not feel sure of yourself when answering questions like these, turn the page and begin with the first frame.

If you were able to get all four answers correct, you may skip to Chapter 3.

♪

quarter

♪ ♪

eighth

one
one-half

one-half

In Chapter 1 we talked about three kinds of notes and three kinds of rests. There are two other kinds of notes we will learn. One of these is the *eighth note* (♪). It looks like the quarter note, except that there is a "flag" attached to the stem. Draw an *eighth note.* _____

From what we have learned about *whole*, *half*, and *quarter* notes, we can guess that an *eighth note* is worth half as many beats as a _____ note.

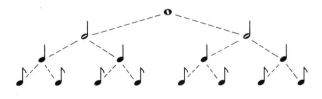

Fill in two of the same kind of note to complete this pattern.

Each of the measures here has three beats. In the second measure, two _____ notes were put in the place of one quarter note.

In this example, each note is worth half the value of the one before it. If the *whole* note is worth four beats, the *half* note is worth two beats, the *quarter* note is worth _____ beat, and the *eighth* note is worth _____ of a beat.

𝅝 𝅗𝅥 ♩ ♪

When the *quarter* note is worth one beat, the *eighth* note is worth _____ beat(s).

26

Draw *one note* which is equal in value to these two notes.

Draw *one note* which would be equal in value to these four notes.

The *top* number of the time signature (meter signature) tells us how many _____ there are in every _____.

beats (counts)
measure

With this time signature, is this measure complete? _____ [yes/no]

Yes
There are two
   beats in the
   measure:

♪ = ½

♪ = ½

♩ = 1

With this time signature, is this measure complete? _____ [yes/no]

No
There are only
   three and one-
   half beats in
   the measure :

▬ = 2

♩ = 1

♪ = ½

The first measure is complete. Draw *one note* which would complete the second measure. _____

27

♪

The first measure is complete. Draw *one note* which would complete the second measure. ________

♪

The first measure is complete. Draw *one note* which would complete the second measure. ________

1. 𝄼
2. 𝄽

Draw a half rest at number 1 and a quarter rest at number 2.

1. ________
2. ________

𝄾

The *rest* that corresponds to an eighth note looks something like a 7. Here is an eighth rest (𝄾). Draw an eighth rest. ________

one-half

If a *quarter* note is worth one beat, an *eighth* will be worth *one-half* a beat, and the *eighth rest* will also be worth ___________ a beat.

𝄾

Complete the second measure with *one rest.* Draw that rest here. ________

𝅗𝅥

The first measure is complete. Draw *one note* which would complete the second measure. ________

Draw *one rest* which would complete the second measure. _______

1. 
2. 
3. 

Draw the following rests:

1. Half rest _______
2. Quarter rest _______
3. Eighth rest _______

(*any order*)

Draw *three rests* which together would complete the second measure. _______, _______, _______

note
one beat

The bottom number of the time signature (meter signature) tells us what kind of a __________ receives __________ __________.

quarter

With this time signature, we know that a(n) __________ note will receive *one* beat.

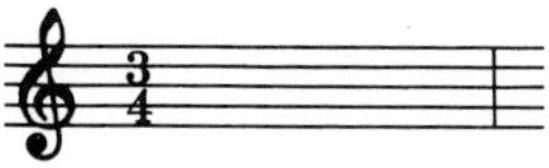

half

With this time signature, we know that a(n) __________ note must receive *one* beat.

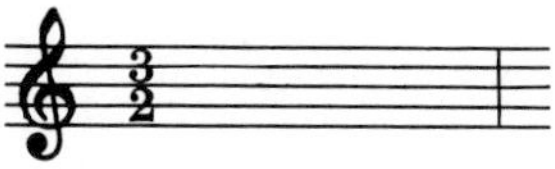

With this signature, the 8 stands for *eighth note*. With this signature the _____ note will receive *one* beat.

In order to save having to write so many "flags" on the eighth notes, composers often "beam" two or more eighth notes together. Complete this pattern.

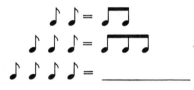

The first measure is complete. Draw *one note* which would complete the second measure. _____

The first measure is complete. Draw *one note* which would complete the second measure. _____

Draw *one rest* which would complete the second measure.

_____

30

In this time signature, the bottom number is _____.
The number 2 stands for *half note*. In this song, the
_____ note will receive *one* beat.

Draw *one note* which would complete the second measure.

_____

Draw *one rest* which would accurately complete the second
measure. _____

Draw *one note* which would accurately complete the second measure. _____

With this time signature, what kind of a *note* would get
one beat? _____ _____ What kind of a *rest*
would get one beat? _____ _____

Draw *one rest* which would complete the second measure.

_____

31

Draw *one note* which would accurately complete the second measure. _____

Draw *two notes* of the same kind which would together complete this second measure. _____

We often see this sign (¢) used as a time signature. When you see this (¢), you call it $\frac{2}{2}$. It is no more complicated than that. If you see a time signature that looks like this (¢), you merely treat it as though the numbers _____ were there.

Draw *one note* which would accurately complete the second measure. _____

There is one other sign that we often see used as a time signature (**c**). Whenever you see this you treat it as though the time signature was $\frac{4}{4}$. This time signature (**c**) is the same as _____.

Draw the following rests:

1. Half rest   _____

2. Quarter rest _____

3. Eighth rest   _____

32

Draw *one rest* which will complete the second measure.

_____

When we see this time signature (**C**), we know that it is the same as _____. When we see this time signature (**¢**), we know that it is the same as _____.

With this time signature (**C**) a(n) _____ note receives *one* beat.

With this time signature (**¢**), a(n) _____ note receives *one* beat.

There is one other kind of note we will learn about. This is a sixteenth note (𝅘𝅥𝅯). It is like the eighth note, except that it has *two* flags instead of one. From what you have learned about the other notes, you can guess that a sixteenth note (𝅘𝅥𝅯) is worth _____ as much as an eighth note.

Sixteenth notes are often *beamed* together like eighth notes. Complete this pattern.

𝅘𝅥𝅯 𝅘𝅥𝅯 = 𝅘𝅥𝅰𝅘𝅥𝅰

𝅘𝅥𝅯 𝅘𝅥𝅯 𝅘𝅥𝅯 𝅘𝅥𝅯 = _____

You have probably noticed that eighth notes have *one* flag, so they require only *one* beam (𝅘𝅥𝅮𝅘𝅥𝅮). Sixteenth notes have two flags (𝅘𝅥𝅯) and they require _____ beams (𝅘𝅥𝅰𝅘𝅥𝅰).

33

quarter

half

one-half

two

Complete this pattern.

♪ ♪ ♪ = ♫♫
♪ ♪ ♪ = ♫♫
♪ ♪ ♪ = ♫♫
♪ ♪ ♪ = _____

Complete this pattern.

♫♫ = ♪ ♪ = ♩
♫♫ = ♪ ♪ = _____

Draw *one note* which is equal in value to these three notes.

_____

♫♫

Draw *one note* which would accurately complete the second measure. _____

If a quarter note (♩) is worth one beat, an eighth note (♪) is worth one-half of a beat and a sixteenth note (♪) is worth _____ of a beat.

one-fourth

Complete this pattern.

𝅝 = _____ beat(s)
𝅗𝅥 = 2 beats
♩ = _____ beat(s)
♪ = ½ beat
♪ = _____ beat(s)

4

1

¼

34

2

½

¼

4

2

½

one-half

three

six

three

Complete this pattern.

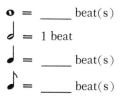

𝅝 = _____ beat(s)

𝅗𝅥 = 1 beat

𝅘𝅥 = _____ beat(s)

𝅘𝅥𝅮 = _____ beat(s)

We will do one more of these. Complete this pattern.

𝅝 = 8 beats

𝅗𝅥 = _____ beat(s)

𝅘𝅥 = _____ beat(s)

𝅘𝅥𝅮 = 1 beat

𝅘𝅥𝅯 = _____ beat(s)

Sometimes you will see a *dot* after a note like this (𝅘𝅥.). The dot *increases* the value of the note by *one-half*. A dot after any note will increase the value of that note by _____.

For example, suppose this note (𝅝) is worth four beats. A *dot* after this note would be worth two beats (half of four). This note (𝅝.), then, would be worth six beats (four plus two). Suppose this note (𝅗𝅥) is worth two beats. A dot after it would be worth one beat (half of two). This note (𝅗𝅥.) is worth a total of _____ beats (two plus one).

This note (𝅝) is worth four beats, so this note (𝅝.) is worth _____ beat(s). (Half again as much.)

This note (𝅗𝅥) is worth two beats. How much is this note (𝅗𝅥.) worth? _____ (The dot makes it worth half again as much.)

35

1½

This note (♩) is worth one beat. How much is this note (♩.) worth? _____ beat(s)

three-fourths

This note (♪) is worth one-half of a beat. How many beats would this note (♪.) be worth? _____ [one-half plus one-fourth]

You *can* look at it this way. Complete this pattern.

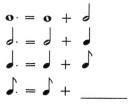

♪

Yes
These notes
total 3 beats:
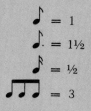
♩. = 1½
♪ = ½
♩ = 1

With this time signature, is this a complete measure? _____ [yes/no]

Yes
These notes
total 6 beats:
♪ = 1
♪. = 1½
♪ = ½
= 3

With this time signature, is this a complete measure? _____ [yes/no]

2
2

Whenever we see this sign (C) in the time signature, we know that it is the same thing as $\frac{4}{4}$. Whenever we see this sign (¢) in the time signature, we know that it is the same thing as _____.

2
2

4
4

*No answer
required.*

Write the numbers which are the same as this time signature (¢). _____ Write the numbers which are the same as this time signature (**c**). _____

You have now learned a great deal about what we call the rhythmical aspect of music. That is, you know a lot about how long or how short the notes and rests should be. The next few questions will give you a chance to check yourself on your new knowledge. Do them carefully and see how you come out.

The first measure is complete. Draw *one rest* which would complete the second measure. _____

The first measure is complete. Draw *one note* which would accurately complete the second measure. _____

The top number of the time signature (meter signature) tells us how many _____ there are in every _____.

beats
measure

The first measure is complete. Draw *one rest* which would accurately complete the second measure. _____

Draw *one note* which would complete the second measure. The first measure is complete. _____

The first measure is complete. Draw *one note* which would accurately complete the second measure. _____

The first measure is complete. Draw *one note* which would accurately complete the second measure. _____

note
one beat

The bottom number of the time signature (meter signature) tells us what kind of a _____ receives _____ _____.

The first measure is complete. Draw *one rest* which would accurately complete the second measure. _____

The first measure is complete. Draw *one note* which would accurately complete the second measure. _____

The Staff

Clefs and Note Names

Chapter 3 is designed to provide you with important information about the names of the notes on the staff and to familiarize you with the treble and bass clefs.

If you wish to check your present knowledge, try to answer this question and then check your answer on the next page. If you are sure that you cannot answer the question, turn the page now.

Criterion Question

Write the letter names for these notes. Answer all parts of the question before checking your answers.

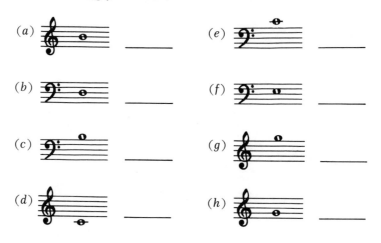

Here are the correct answers to the criterion question on the preceding page:

(*a*)	B	(*e*)	C
(*b*)	D	(*f*)	E
(*c*)	B	(*g*)	G
(*d*)	C	(*h*)	G

If you missed an answer, or if you do not feel sure of yourself when
answering questions like this, turn the page and begin with the first
frame.

If you were able to get all eight of the answers right, you may skip
to Chapter 4.

The symbols used on a printed page to represent musical sounds are called *notes*. Here are four different kinds of

notes

_____.

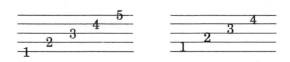

Notes are written on a *staff* which has *five lines* and *four spaces*, as shown.

five

four

A staff will always have _____ [number] lines and _____ [number] spaces.

If a note is written as in (*a*) we say that it is in the *first* line. When a note is written as in (*b*), we say that it is in the *second* line. In which line was the note in (*c*)

fourth

placed?

(*a*) (*b*) (*c*)

If a note appears as in (*a*) we say that it is in the second

fourth

space. In which space was the note in (*b*) placed?

(*a*) (*b*)

first

third, fifth

In which lines do these notes appear? The _____ line, the _____ line, and the _____ line.

Write a whole note in each of the four spaces on the staff. The first two are given.

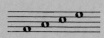

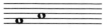

42

Write a note in each of the five lines of the staff. The first two are given.

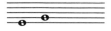

When we listen to music, we often hear both *high* sounds and *low* sounds. These *low* and *high* sounds are represented by the notes on the staff. The higher the note is on the staff, the higher it will sound to the ear. The lower the note is on the staff, the _____ it will sound to the ear.

lower

Which one of these notes would sound *lower* to a listener, note *a* or note *b*? _____

(a)   (b)

note *b*
It is the lower one on the staff.

Which one of these notes would sound *higher* to a listener, note *a* or note *b*? _____

(a)   (b)

note *b*
It is up higher on the staff.

If a composer needs to write a note which is higher than the fifth line of the staff, he may write it as shown at (a), on top of the staff. This note was written in the *space on top of the staff*. If he were to write a note below the first line, he would write it as shown at (b). This note is in the first space b_____w the staff.

below

(a)   (b)

43

Now, what happens if a composer needs to write a note even lower than at (*a*)? He is out of lines and spaces! He just adds a little *ledger line* as at (*b*) and then writes in the note as at (*c*). The extra lines added below, or above, the staff are called _____ lines.

ledger

(*a*)   (*b*)   (*c*)

ledger
ledger

This staff has two _____ lines above and one _____ line below.

Letter names are often applied to the lines and spaces of the staff. In music, it is quite simple, however, because only the *first seven* letters of the alphabet are used. Write the seven letters of the alphabet that are used in music:

A, B, C, D, E, F, G

_____ , _____ , _____ , _____ , _____ , _____ ,

_____ .

Clef signs, placed at the beginning of the staff, determine the letter names of the lines and spaces. We will work with only two *clef signs.* One *clef sign* appears on the staff as at (*a*), and the other _____ sign appears as at (*b*).

clef

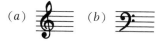

(*a*)   (*b*)

The clef sign that appears at (*a*) is called the *treble clef.* The one at (*b*) is called the *bass clef.* The two _____ signs we will work with are the _____ clef and the bass clef.

clef
treble

(*a*)   (*b*)

In the treble clef, the letter names of the lines and spaces are *always* as shown. (Notice that when you get to G, you start again with A.) The name of the note in the first *line* is _____.

E F G A B C D E F

E

Whenever the treble clef is used in this manner, the name of the note in the first line will *always* be _____.

E

E

A note is given a letter name according to the line or space in which it appears. The note on the first line here is _____. The *next note above* E falls in a _____ [line/space].

E, space

Name the seven letters used in music: _____, _____, _____, _____, _____, _____, _____.

A, B,
C, D, E, F, G

If the note in the first line is called E, the note which comes *after* E, in the space above, would be called _____.

F

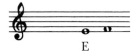

E

Fill in the missing letter names for each of the notes shown. (Remember that when you get to G, you start again with A.)

F, A, E   E __ G __ B C D __ F

Fill in the missing letter names for each of the notes on this staff. (When you get to G, you must start again with A.)

G, A, B   E F __ __ __ C D E F

Now, if you have done fairly well so far, try this. What is the name of the note in the second line? _____ (Don't forget that there is a space between these two notes!)

G

E

When the treble clef is used, the name of the note in the first line is always _____. Fill in the names of the notes shown.

E

E, F, G, A   __ __ __ __

When the treble clef is used, the name of the note in the first line is always _____. Fill in the names of the notes called for.

E

G, F   __   __

Fill in the names of the notes shown.

E, G, C   — — —

Write in the names of these notes.

F, A, E   — — —

Write the letter name for each of these notes.

1. D   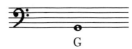   1. _____

2. B   2. _____

3. C   3. _____

E

G

When the treble clef is used, the name of the note in the first line is always _____. However, when the *bass* clef (shown) is used, the name of the note in the first line is always _____.

G

Letter names for the notes in the *bass clef* will always appear as shown below. When the bass clef is used the name of the note in the first line is always _____.

G   A   B   C   D   E   F   G   A

E

G

G, C, F

G
E

G, A, B

G, D, G

1. F

2. C

3. G

When the treble clef [see (*a*)] is used, the name of the note in the first line is _____. When the bass clef [see (*b*)] is used, however, the name of the note in the first line is always _____.

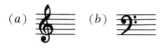

Fill in the letter names of the notes on the staff. (Remember that when you get to G, you start again with A.) Write names for only the three notes indicated.

___ A ___ E ___

When the *bass* clef is used, the name of the note in the first line is _____. When the *treble* clef is used, the name of the note in the first line is _____.

Name these notes in the bass clef.

___ ___ ___

Name these notes.

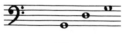

___ ___ ___

Name each of the notes shown.

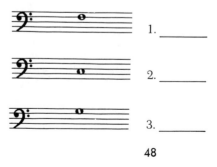

1. _____

2. _____

3. _____

48

G, B, D

*Did you get
caught by the
clef sign?
Watch the
clefs. They can
trick you!*

G, B, G

D, C

B, C

C

Name these notes.

Here are a few more. Name these.

Fill in these note names. Notice the ledger line.

A   G   F   E   __   __

Here is a ledger line in the bass clef. Name these notes.

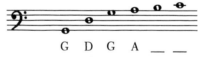

G   D   G   A   __   __

Now, take a look at how the two clefs look when placed one under the other. This is the way they usually look in piano music. Notice that the ledger line above the bass clef and the ledger line below the treble clef are the *same* note. The name of this note is _____.

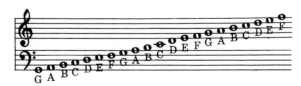

49

C

The name of this note, one ledger line above the bass clef, is _____. (Look back at the illustration for the preceding frame, if necessary.)

C

Name this note, one ledger line below the treble clef.

_____

C

Name this note.

Fill in the letter names of the notes where they are called for.

A, B, C, D

G _ _ _ _ E

Here are a few more for practice. Write the letter names. Watch the clef!

1. B   3. B

2. D   4. C

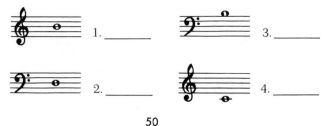

1. _____   3. _____

2. _____   4. _____

Write these letter names. Watch the clef!

1. _____   3. _____

2. _____   4. _____

1. C   3. G

2. E   4. G

Name these notes and see what word you have.

— — —

A G E

What word do you get from this one?

— — — —

F A D E

Try this word. Watch the clef!

— — —

E G G

Here is one more word.

— — —

B E D

Now, give yourself a final check on these. Be careful of the last one!

1. G   3. F

2. E   4. A

1. _____   3. _____

2. _____   4. _____

51

The Piano
Keyboard

53

This chapter will acquaint you with the piano keyboard and the relationship between the keys of the keyboard and the notes on the staff. In this chapter, and in those that follow, you will find that questions on material studied previously will appear unexpectedly from time to time. This, of course, is a check on your learning. If you find that you are missing one particular kind of question each time it appears, you may wish to return to the chapter which deals with that question, in order to refresh your memory.

Criterion Questions

1. The note on this staff could be sounded by striking key number _____ on the keyboard shown. The name of this note is _____.

2. The note on this staff could be sounded by striking key number _____ on the keyboard. The name of this note is _____.

3. The note on this staff could be sounded by striking key number _____ on the keyboard. The name of this note is _____.

4. The note on this staff could be sounded by striking key number _____ on the keyboard. The name of this note is _____.

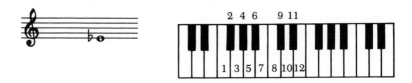

Here are the correct answers to the criterion questions on the preceding page:

   1. 12, E
   2.　1, F
   3.　9, C♯
   4. 11, E♭

If you missed an answer, or if you do not feel sure of yourself when answering questions like these, turn the page and begin with the first frame.

If you were able to get all eight answers correct, you may skip to the beginning of Chapter 5.

A small portion of a piano keyboard is pictured here. Some of the keys are white and others are black. In *this* picture, there are _____ [number] white keys and _____ [number] black keys.

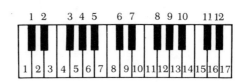

Some of the keys on the keyboard are _____ [color] and others are _____ [color].

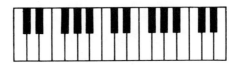

The keys of the piano keyboard have letter names just as the lines and spaces have letter names. The *first seven* letters of the alphabet are used for the keyboard. Name these seven letters: _____, _____, _____, _____, _____, _____, _____.

The first seven letters of the alphabet are used to name the keys on the keyboard as shown here. Notice that when you get to G, you start again with A. Name the white key at the arrow. _____

Name the key at the arrow. _____

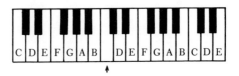

E

B, G

Here, the arrows are pointing to which keys? _____,
_____, _____ (Remember that when you get to G, you
start again with A.)

Just to be sure that you haven't forgotten what you learned
earlier, check yourself on these. Write the letter names for
the notes shown. (Watch the clef!)

1. F   3. D

2. A   4. D

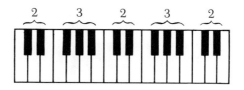

1. _____   3. _____

2. _____   4. _____

A careful look at a piano keyboard will show you that
the *black* keys are always placed in groups of two and

three

two

three. This section of a keyboard shows _____ [num-
ber] groups of two and _____ [number] groups of
three.

The key to the left of a group of two is always C. The key

F

to the left of a group of three is always _____.

C
F

The key to the left of a group of two is always _____.

The key to the left of a group of three is always _____.

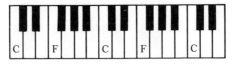

The first measure is complete. Draw *one rest* which would complete the second measure. _____

C

To which key is the arrow pointing? _____

C, F

The arrows are pointing to _____ and _____.

C, F

The arrows are pointing to _____ and _____.

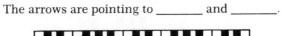

F, G

The arrows are pointing to _____ and _____.

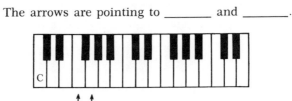

C, C, F

The arrows are pointing to _____, _____, and _____.

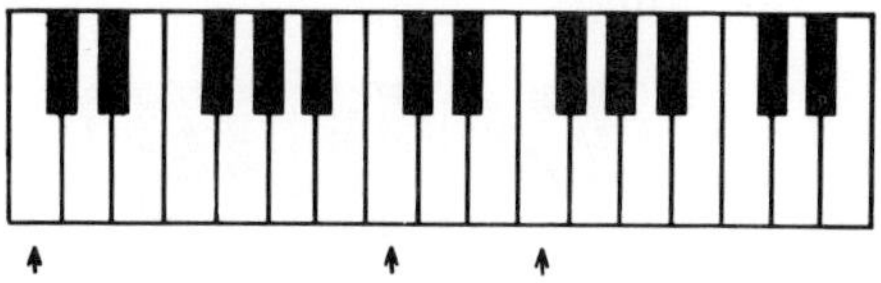

B

The arrow is pointing to _____.

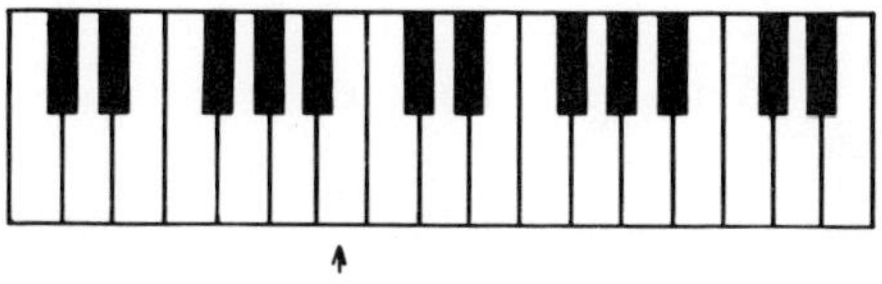

F

The arrow is pointing to _____.

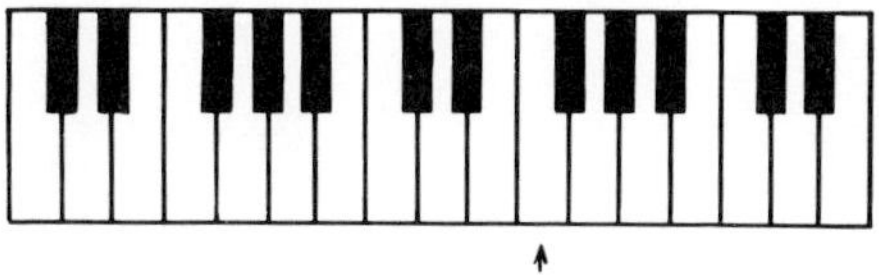

A

The arrow is pointing to _____.

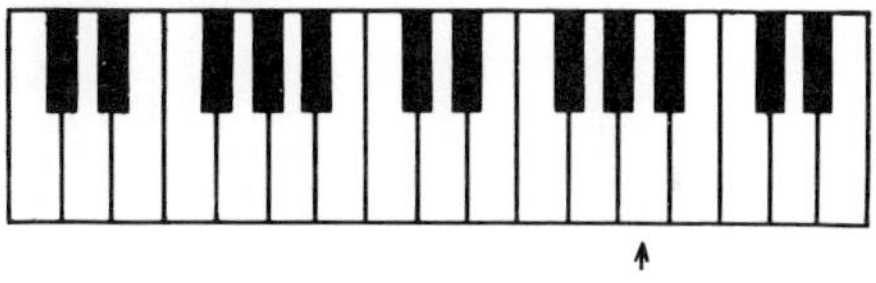

E

The arrow is pointing to _____.

D

The arrow is pointing to _____.

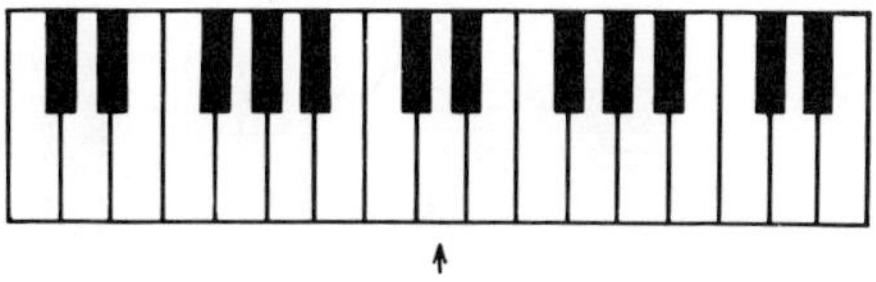

Here is a smaller section of a keyboard. The arrow is pointing to _____.

G

Here is another check on your knowledge of note names. Write the letter names for these notes.

1. C   3. C

2. C   4. C

1. _____

3. _____

2. _____

4. _____

What is the letter name of the note on the staff? _____
What key would you strike on the keyboard to sound the note on the staff? _____ [number]

F

5

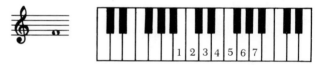

The note on the staff could be sounded by striking key number _____ on the keyboard.

3

The note on the staff could be sounded by striking key number _____ on the keyboard. (Watch the clef!)

1

The note on the staff could be sounded by striking key number _____ on the keyboard.

The note on the staff could be sounded by striking key number _____ on the keyboard.

You now know quite a bit about the white keys on the piano. Let's look more closely at the *black* keys. In order to name these, we make use of two symbols—one of which is the *sharp* (♯). Draw a sharp. _____

raise

A sharp is used in music to *raise* a note one half step— that is, to make it sound a little higher. If we place a sharp (♯) in front of a note, it will r_____ the note one half step.

2

Now this works out very nicely on the piano keyboard because there is exactly one half step from *any* key on the keyboard to its *nearest neighbor*. The nearest key above number 1 is number 2. So, there is a half step from 1 to _____.

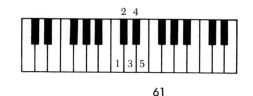

61

So, it is as simple as this: The key at number 1 is C. The black key just above C is one half step higher, so we call this black key C♯ (pronounced C sharp). The key at number 2 is D. The black key just above D would be called _____.

D♯ (or D sharp)

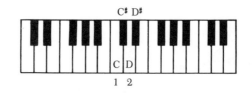

C♯ (or C sharp)

What is the name of the black key at the arrow? _____

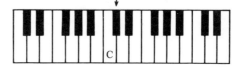

D♯ (or D sharp)

What is the name of the black key at the arrow? _____

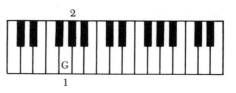

G♯ (or G sharp)

The name of the key at number 1 is G. What is the name of the key at number 2? _____

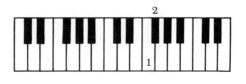

F

F♯

What is the name of the key at number 1? _____ What is the name of the key at number 2? _____

A
A♯

3

G♯

E, A♯, F♯

F♯

What is the name of the key at number 1? _____ What is the name of the key at number 2? _____

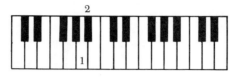

The note on the staff could be sounded by striking key number _____ on the keyboard.

What is the key at the arrow? _____

Name the notes at the arrows. _____, _____, _____

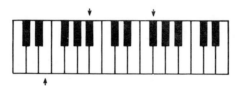

This will give you an idea of how the notes for the black keys look on the staff. The note at number 1 is called G. The note at number 2 is called G♯ (pronounced G sharp). The note at number 3 is called _____.

63

The note on staff *a* could be sounded by striking key number 2 on the keyboard. What number key would you strike to sound the note on staff *b*? _____

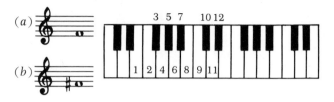

The note on the staff could be sounded by striking key number _____ on the keyboard.

The note on the staff could be sounded by striking key number _____ on the keyboard.

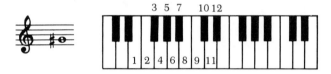

The note on the staff could be sounded by striking key number _____ on the keyboard.

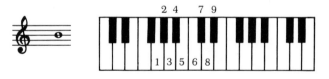

Did you see the bass clef?

The note on the staff could be sounded by striking key number _____ on the keyboard.

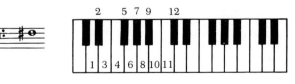

64

2

The note on the staff could be sounded by striking key number _____ on the keyboard.

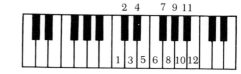

4

The note on the staff could be sounded by striking key number _____ on the keyboard.

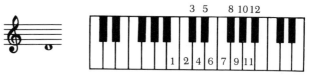

5

The note on the staff could be sounded by striking key number _____ on the keyboard.

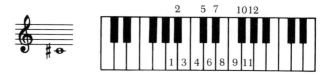

12

The note on the staff could be sounded by striking key number _____ on the keyboard.

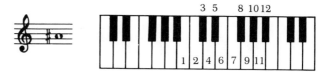

8

The note on the staff could be sounded by striking key number _____ on the keyboard.

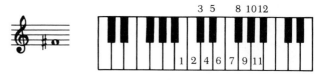

You are now getting to know the keyboard quite well. The other symbol used in naming the black keys is the flat (♭). Draw a flat. _____

♭

A flat (♭) is used in music to *lower* a note one half step—that is, to make it sound a little *lower*. If we place a flat in front of a note, it will l_____ the note one half step.

lower

The keys on the keyboard are located one half step apart. The closest key *below* number 7 is number 6. Key number 7 is called A, so key number 6 can be called A♭ (pronounced A flat). Key number 5 is called _____, so key number 4 can be called _____.

G
G♭

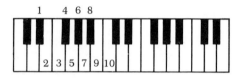

In the English language there are words such as "bear" and "bare" that sound alike but are spelled differently. This happens in music, too. The black key at the arrow (a half step above C) can be called C♯. The very same black key (a half step *below* D) can also be called _____♭.

D♭

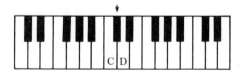

The key at the arrow could be called G♯ (half step above G) or _____♭ (a half step below A).

A♭

66

D
E
E♭

A
B
B♭

G♭

D♭

𝅗𝅥

The name of the key at number 1 is _____. The name of the key at number 3 is _____. One name for the key at number 2 is D♯. What is another name for the key at number 2? _____♭

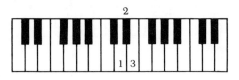

The name of the key at number 1 is _____. The name of the key at number 3 is _____. One name for the key at number 2 is A♯. What is another name for the key at number 2? _____

One name for the key at the arrow is F♯. What is another name for this key? _____

One name for the key at the arrow is C♯. What is another name for this key? _____

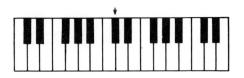

The first measure is complete. Draw *one note* which would complete the second measure. _____

One name for the key at the arrow is G♯. What is another name for this key? _____

One name for the key at the arrow is E♭. Write another name for the same key. _____♯

One name for the note at the arrow is B♭. What is another name for this same note? _____

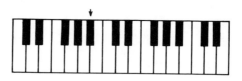

Write two correct names for the key at the arrow. _____,

_____

The top number of the time signature (meter signature) tells us how many _____ there are in every _____.

Write two correct names for this key. _____, _____

A♭

D♯

A♯

C♯
D♭
(either order)

beats
measure

G♯, A♭
(either order)

68

A♯, B♭
(*either order*)

D♭

C♯

G♭

G♭

D♯

Write two correct names for this key. _____, _____

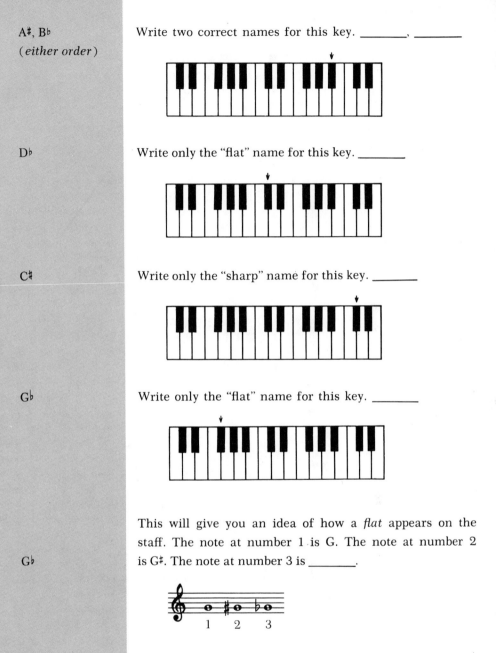

Write only the "flat" name for this key. _____

Write only the "sharp" name for this key. _____

Write only the "flat" name for this key. _____

This will give you an idea of how a *flat* appears on the staff. The note at number 1 is G. The note at number 2 is G♯. The note at number 3 is _____.

The note at number 1 is D. The note at number 2 is D♭ (pronounced D flat). The note at number 3 is _____.

69

C

Write the name of the note at the arrow. _____

F

Write the name of the note at the arrow. _____

D♭ or C♯

Write the name of the note at the arrow. _____

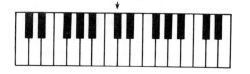

F♯ or G♭

Write the name of the note at the arrow. _____

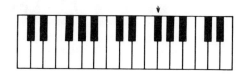

B or C♭

Write the name of the note at the arrow. _____

D♯ or E♭

Write the name of the note at the arrow. _____

The bottom number of a time signature (meter signature) tells us what kind of a _____ receives _____ _____.

You have now learned a great deal about the piano keyboard and its relationship to the notes on the staff. The next nine questions will give you some practice in using what you have learned so far in this program. Be careful and find out just how expert you are. Watch out for those clefs!

The note on the staff could be sounded by striking key number _____ on the keyboard. What is the name of this note? _____

The note on the staff could be sounded by striking key number _____ on the keyboard. What is the name of this note? _____

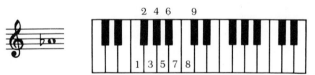

The note on the staff could be sounded by striking key number _____ on the keyboard. What is the name of this note? _____

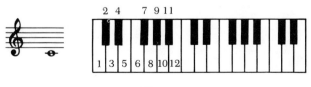

2
C♯
*Did you see
the clef?*

The note on the staff could be sounded by striking key number _____ on the keyboard. What is the name of this note? _____

7
E♭

The note on the staff could be sounded by striking key number _____ on the keyboard. What is the name of this note? _____

1
G

The note on the staff could be sounded by striking key number _____ on the keyboard. What is the name of this note? _____

12
B♭

The note on the staff could be sounded by striking key number _____ on the keyboard. What is the name of this note? _____

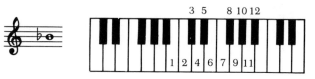

6
F

9
F#

The note on the staff could be sounded by striking key number _____ on the keyboard. What is the name of this note? _____

The note on the staff could be sounded by striking key number _____ on the keyboard. What is the name of this note? _____

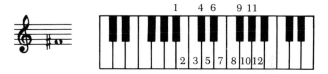

CHAPTER 5

Intervals

Whole Steps; Half Steps

In this chapter you will be introduced to the concept of half steps and whole steps, and you will learn how to write these on a staff. If you would like to try a few before you start, answer the following questions. If you cannot answer the questions, turn the page now.

Criterion Questions

1. Write on the staff a note which is one whole step above each note given.

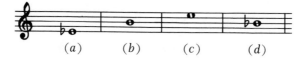

      (*a*)   (*b*)   (*c*)   (*d*)

2. Write on the staff a note which is one half step above each note given.

      (*a*)   (*b*)

Check your answers on the next page after you have completed both questions.

Here are the correct answers to the criterion questions on the preceding page. These are the notes that you should have written on the staff. Be sure that yours are *exactly* like these before counting them correct.

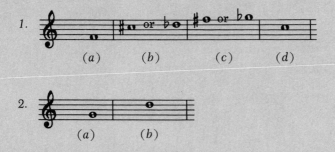

If you missed an answer, or if you feel uncertain about your answers, turn the page and begin with the first frame.

If you were able to get all six answers correct, you may skip to the beginning of Chapter 6.

We have already said that the keys on a piano keyboard are one half step apart. In other words, the distance or interval from C to C♯ on this keyboard is a half step. Knowing this, we can also figure that the interval between F and F♯ is also a _____ step.

half

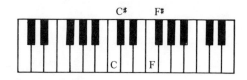

The interval from any key on the keyboard to its nearest neighbor is a *half step*. The interval from key number 2 to key number 1 is a half step. The interval from key number 2 to key number 3 is a _____ _____.

half step

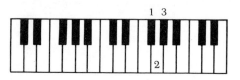

The interval from any key on the keyboard to its closest neighbor, *either above or below*, is always one _____ _____.

half
step

The closest neighbor is always one half step away. The nearest neighbor *below* G♯ is G. The interval between G♯ and G, then _____ [is/is not] one half step.

is

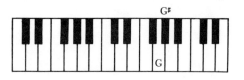

The interval from C to C♯ is a half step. Is the interval from C♯ to D also a half step? _____ [yes/no]

yes

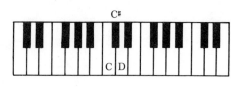

78

C

C

The nearest neighbor to B, on the lower side, is B♭. The nearest neighbor to B, on the upper side, is _____. There is one half step between B and its upper neighbor which is _____.

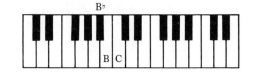

F

There is one half step between E and its upper neighbor which is _____.

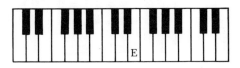

half steps

If there is an interval of *one* half step between D and D♯, then there must be *two* h_____ s_____ between D and E.

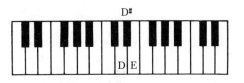

two

If there is an interval of *one* half step between G and G♯, there must be _____ [number] half steps between G and A.

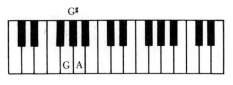

two
one

How many half steps are there between F and G? _____ [number] How many from F to F♯? _____ [number]

one
two

How many half steps are there between A and B♭? _____ [number] How many between A and B? _____ [number]

one

Now, from what we know about arithmetic, we might guess that two half steps will be equal to _____ [number] whole step(s).

one

The interval from F to G is two half steps or _____ [number] whole step(s).

one

The interval from G to A is _____ [number] whole step(s).

half

The interval from C♯ to D is one _____ step.

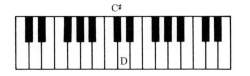

The first measure is complete. Draw *one note* which would accurately complete the second measure. _____

o

whole

The interval from D to C is one _____ step.

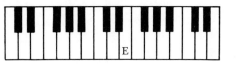

half

The interval from E♭ to E is one _____ step.

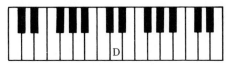

half

The interval from E to F is one _____ step.

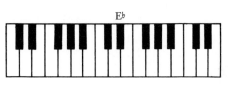

whole

The interval from F♯ to G♯ is one _____ step.

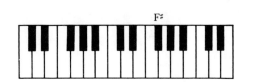

Try one more. The interval from B to C is one _____ step.

Try a few this way now. The interval between the arrows is one _____ step.

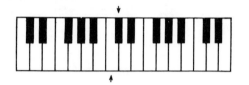

The interval between the arrows is one _____ step.

The first measure is complete. Draw *one rest* which would complete the second measure. _____

The interval between the arrows is one _____ step.

82

half

half

half

C

F, C

The interval between the arrows is one _____ step.

Find E on the keyboard. What is the interval between E and F? One _____ step.

Find B on the keyboard. What is the interval between B and C? One _____ step.

Looking at the keyboard, we can see that there is always a black key between the white keys *except* between E and F and between B and _____.

We will always find a black key between the white keys, except between E and _____ and between B and _____.

F, C

There is a *whole* step between white keys *except* between E and _____ and between B and _____ where there is a *half* step.

F

There is a half step between E and _____ because there is no black key between these two white keys.

C

We also know that there is a half step between B and _____ because there is no black key between these two white keys.

E, F, B
C

There is always one whole step between white keys except between _____ and _____ and between _____ and _____ where there is a half step.

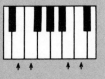

half

What is the interval between E and F? One _____ step.

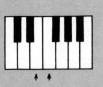

84

half

What is the interval between C and C♯? One _____ step.

whole

What is the interval between G and A? One _____ step.

half

The interval between B and C is one _____ step.

half

The interval between G♯ and A is one _____ step.

half

The interval between A♭ and A is one _____ step.

half

The interval between B♭ and A is one _____ step.

85

half

The interval between A♯ and A is one _____ step.

whole

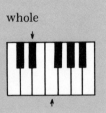

The interval between E♭ and F is one _____ step. Be careful of this one!

whole

The interval between B♭ and C is one _____ step.

whole

The interval between F♯ and E is one _____ step. Be careful of this one, too!

half

The interval between D and D♯ is one _____ step.

Let's try a few this way. Name the key on the keyboard which is one *half* step *above* C. _____

C♯ or D♭

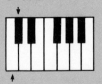

86

F♯ or G♭

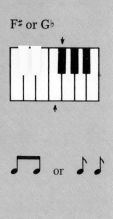

Name the key on the keyboard which is one *half* step *above* F. _____

 or ♪ ♪

The first measure is complete. Draw *two notes* of the same kind which together would complete the second measure. _____

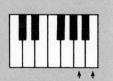

G

Name the key on the keyboard which is one *half* step *below* G♯. _____

A

Name the key which is one *whole* step *above* G. _____

A

Name the key which is one whole step below B. _____

A♯ or B♭

Name the key which is one half step above A. _____

Now, let's look at how this matter of half steps works on the staff. Keeping the keyboard in mind, do you think the interval between these two notes is a *half* step or a *whole* step? A _____ step.

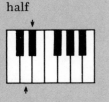
half

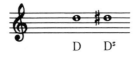

D   D♯

Is the interval between these two notes a half step or a whole step? A _____ step.

half

F

The bottom number of the time signature (meter signature) tells us what kind of a _____ receives _____ _____.

note
one beat

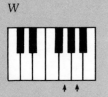

The first measure is complete. Draw *one note* which would complete the second measure. _____

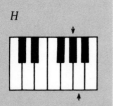

This interval is a _____ step. (To save time, just write *H* for half and *W* for whole.)

W

This interval is a _____ step.

H

88

H

This interval is a _____ step.

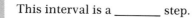

H

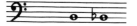

This interval is a _____ step.

Did you see the clef sign?

beats
measure

The top number of the time signature (meter signature) tells us how many _____ there are in every _____.

H

This interval is a _____ step.

H

This interval is a _____ step.

H

This interval is a _____ step.

89

H

This interval is a _____ step.

W

This interval is a _____ step.

W

This interval is a _____ step.

W

This interval is a _____ step.

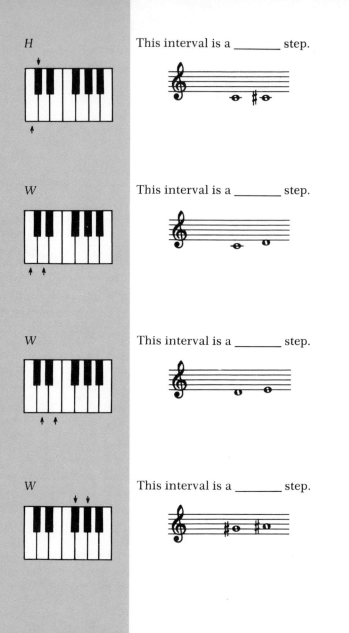

So far, so good! Now you will learn to write intervals on the staff. Write on the staff a note which is one *whole* step *above* the G which is given. This, of course, will be an A. Write it in.

Write on the staff a note which is one whole step above the note given.

When we write E flat this way, E♭, the flat comes *after* the letter E. With a note on the staff, however, the sharp or flat always comes *in front* of the note. Look at these two B♭'s written on the staffs at (*a*). Write a sharp by the note on the staff at (*b*) which will make the note C♯. Be sure to place the sharp *before* the note.

This would be

wrong:

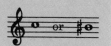

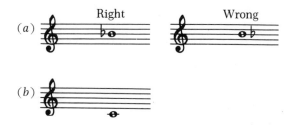

Write on the staff a note which is one half step above the given note.

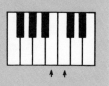

Write on the staff a note which is one half step above the given note.

Write on the staff a note which is one half step above the given note.

Write on the staff a note which is one whole step above the given note.

Write on the staff a note which is one whole step above the given note.

Did you see the clef?

Write on the staff a note which is one whole step above the note given.

Write on the staff a note which is one whole step above the note given.

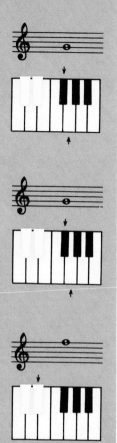

Write on the staff a note which is one half step above the note given.

Write on the staff a note which is one half step above the note given.

Write on the staff a note which is one whole step above the note given.

Write on the staff a note which is one whole step above the note given.

CHAPTER 6

Major Scales
and Key Signatures

In this chapter, you will learn what key signatures are, why they are used, and how to identify the major key in which a song is written by looking at the key signature. You will also learn about the construction of major scales and how to find or identify a note on any step of a major scale.

In order to check your present knowledge, you may want to attempt the following questions. After completing all parts of the questions, check your answers on the next page. If you are sure that you cannot answer these questions, turn the page now.

Criterion Questions

1. Under each of the key signatures, write the name of the major key with which it would be used.

(a) _____   (b) _____   (c) _____

(d) _____   (e) _____   (f) _____

2. (a) This note is scale step number _____ in the major scale of this key.

(b) This note is scale step number _____ in the major scale of this key.

(c) This note is scale step number _____ in the major scale of this key.

Here are the correct answers to the criterion questions on the preceding page:

1. (*a*) B♭   (*b*) G♭   (*c*) B
   (*d*) G   (*e*) C   (*f*) F

2. (*a*) 7
   (*b*) 8 or 1
   (*c*) 3

If you missed any of the answers, or if you do not feel comfortable about dealing with this information, turn the page and begin with the first frame.

If you were able to get all nine answers correct, you may skip to the beginning of Chapter 7.

C

This is a C scale. It begins on C and ends on _____.

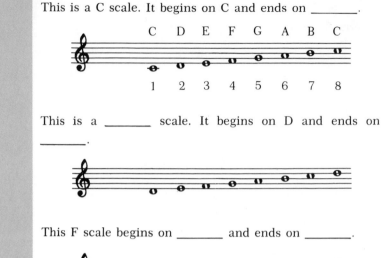

D

D

This is a _____ scale. It begins on D and ends on _____.

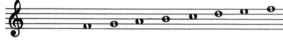

F, F

This F scale begins on _____ and ends on _____.

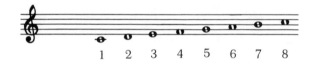

8

Scale step number 1 is C. Scale step number _____ is also C.

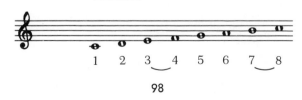

Scales form the basis for most of our music. You will learn about two kinds of scales—*major* scales and *minor* scales. We will save the *minor* scales until later. Right

major

now we will talk about the _____ scales.

Major scales are distinguished from other kinds of scales by the arrangement of half steps and whole steps within the scale. From what you know of whole and half steps, it is easy to see that there is a whole step between each of the notes in this scale *except* between numbers 3 and

4, 8

_____ and 7 and _____.

half

is not

4

8

A major scale always has h_____ steps between numbers 3 and 4 of the scale and between numbers 7 and 8 of the scale.

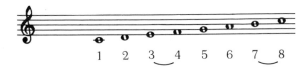

This C scale (*a*) is a *major* scale with half steps between 3 and 4 and between 7 and 8. This F scale (*b*) _____ [is/is not] a major scale. (Notice where the half steps come.)

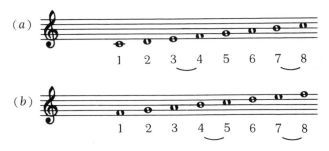

In order to have a *major* scale, the half steps must come between numbers 3 and _____ and between numbers 7 and 8.

Now, if we wish to make the *F scale* at (*a*) into an *F major scale*, all we do is place a flat in front of note B and we have a *major* scale with half steps between 3 and 4 and between 7 and _____ [see (*b*)].

BALLOU LIBRARY
BUENA VISTA COLLEGE
75384 STORM LAKE, IOWA 50588

F

In order to make this G *major* scale into a G *major* scale, we must place a sharp in front of the note _____ so we will have the half steps in the right places.

1   2   3   4   5   6   7   8

F, C

In order to make this D scale into a *major* scale, we must place sharps in front of the notes _____ and _____ in order to have the half steps in the right places.

flats

Any scale can be made into a *major* scale by using sharps or f_____ to arrange the half steps and whole steps in the correct order.

B

If a composer wishes to write a melody based on the F major scale, he will place a flat in front of the note _____ when it appears in the song.

sharp

If a composer wishes to write a song which is based on the D major scale, he will place a _____ in front of the notes F and C every time they appear in his song.

100

F

C, G, D

(*any order*)

F

F

F

key

If a composer wishes to write a song based on the major scale of E, he will have to place a sharp in front of _____, _____, _____, and _____ whenever these notes occur in his song.

When a composer writes a song based on the G major scale, he will generally place a sharp in front of _____ every time the note _____ appears in his song.

As an example of what we have just been talking about, here is a little song based on the G major scale. The note _____ was sharped every time it appeared.

Song

G major scale

Now if a composer has a very long piece of music to write out, all this writing of sharps (or flats) could become quite a job. In order to avoid the continuous writing of sharps or flats, composers make use of a *key signature*. The _____ signature saves much work for the composer and makes the music easier to read because it is less cluttered.

101

In order to see how the key signature works, look at the same little song first *without* a key signature (*a*) and then *with* a key signature (*b*). By placing the sharp in the F line at the beginning of the song, the composer tells you that every time the note _____ appears, it must be sharped.

F

If a composer writes a key signature like this one, he is telling you that the note F must be sharped whenever it appears—whether in the fifth line or in the _____ [number] space.

first

In this key signature, sharps appear in the fifth line which is F and the third space which is _____.

C

With this key signature, we know that the notes _____ and _____ must be sharped no matter when or where they appear in the song.

F
C

In this key signature, flats appear in the third line and in the fourth space. From this, we know that the notes _____ and _____ must be flatted whenever they occur in this song.

B, E

The top number of the *time* signature (meter signature) tells us how many _____ there are in every _____.

beats
measure

What notes would have to be flatted with this key signature? _____, _____, and _____

B, E, A

What notes would have to be sharped with this key signature? _____, _____, and _____

F, C, G

What note would have to be flatted with this key signature? _____ With this key signature, the name of the note on the staff would have to be _____.

B
B♭ or B flat

With this key signature, we know that the note _____ must be sharped whenever it appears. The name of the note on the staff must be _____.

F
F♯ or F sharp

B♭, E♭, E♭

Name these notes. _____ _____ _____

F♯, C♯, F♯

Name these notes. _____ _____ _____

♪

The first measure is complete. Draw *one note* which would complete the second measure. _____

F, B♭, E♭

Name these notes. _____ _____ _____

E, C♯

Name these notes. Look carefully at the key signature!
_____ _____

B, E♯

There is no sharp for B, but the last sharp on the right turns all E's into E♯.

We will try one more like this. Name these notes. Be careful of this one! _____ _____

104

We have seen that there are eight steps in a major scale that go up something like stair steps. In the F major scale, what is the letter name of the sixth scale step? _____

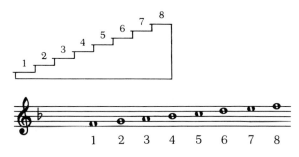

In this G major scale, what is the letter name of the seventh scale step? _____

This is a D major scale. It begins on D and ends on _____.

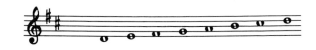

This is a(n) _____ major scale. It begins on _____ and ends on _____.

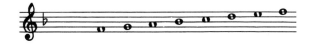

This is a(n) _____ major scale. What is the third scale step? _____

105

Look carefully at the key signature before answering this question. What scale is this? It is a(n) _____ scale. The fourth scale step is _____.

Eb
Ab

Again, be very careful of this one. What is this scale? It is a(n) _____ major scale. The fifth scale step is

_____.

Db
Ab

G is step number 2 in this scale. What is step number 1?

_____

F

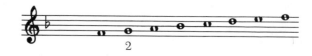

If G is step number 4 in this scale, _____ is step number 3. (Watch the key signature!)

F#

This is the key signature for an F major scale. The first step of this scale would be _____. The fourth step of the scale will be _____.

F
Bb

106

Eb

Ab

A

Eb

G

Bb

ɤ

This is the key signature for an Eb major scale. The first step of the scale will be _____ and the fourth step of the scale will be _____.

The D on the staff is the fourth step in this scale. What is the first step? _____

The Aᵇ on this staff is the fourth scale step. What is the first step in this scale? _____

The F♯ on this staff is the seventh step in the scale. What would scale step number 8 be? _____

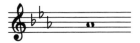

The note on the staff is the seventh step in the scale. What would the eighth scale step be? _____ Watch the key signature!

The first measure is complete. Draw *one rest* which would complete the second measure. _____

The note on the staff is the fourth step in the scale. What would scale step number 1 be? _____

The note on the staff is the seventh step in the scale. What would the eighth step be? _____ Now, we know that steps 1 and 8 are always the same, so what is step number 1 in this scale? _____

Earlier we said that the half steps and whole steps must be in a certain arrangement in order to have a *major* scale. To get this arrangement, the composer may place sharps or flats in front of certain notes, or he may simply use a _____ signature.

Actually, there is a separate key signature for each of the major scales. We usually can tell which major scale was used for a particular song merely by looking at the _____ signature.

When we say that a song is in the "key of F," we are really saying that this song was written using the notes of the F major scale. A song in the *key of G* is written making use of the notes in the _____ major scale.

The key signature for the F major scale is also the key signature for the key of _____.

A key signature for the E♭ major scale is also the key signature for the key of _____.

108

A♭

D

D

key

key

G

F

E♭

key

Now, we usually can tell in what *key* a song is written (or on what major scale the song is written) by looking at the _____ signature.

Db

If a key signature has flats, we must look for the last flat on the right. In this key signature, the name of the last flat on the right is _____.

Ab

Having located the last flat on the right, we call it scale step number 4 and then count down to number 1. The name of scale step number 1 is Ab and *this is the name of the key.* A key signature of four flats is the key signature for the major key of _____.

4   3   2   1

Ab
Eb

Eb

In this key signature, the name of the last flat on the right is _____. Call this step 4 and count down to 1. The name of step 1 is _____. We know then, that the key signature of three flats is always the key signature for the major key of _____.

4   1

To put it all together now:

1. Find the last flat on the right.
2. Call it scale step 4 and count down to 1.
3. Scale step number _____ is the name of the key.

1

Gb

Db

Db

F

F

Eb

Ab

Gb

8

What is the name of the last flat on the right? _____
What is the name of scale step number 1? _____ A
key signature of five flats is always the key signature for
the major key of _____.

Here, there is only one flat, so the name of both the *first*
flat and the *last* is B. What is scale step number 1? _____
This is the key signature for the major key of _____.

What is the major key name for the key signature? _____

What is the major key name for this key signature?

_____

What is the major key name for this key signature?

_____

Now, if our key signature has *sharps*, we call the last sharp
on the right the *seventh* scale step and count *up* to 8. Step
8 is always the same as step 1, so either step 1 or step
_____ can name the key.

D♯

E, E

The name of the last sharp on the right is _____. Call this step 7 and count up to 8. The name of step 8 is _____. The name of the key is _____.

D

This is the key signature for the major key of _____.

A

This is the key signature for the major key of _____.

B

This is the key signature for the major key of _____.

Write the major key name for these two key signatures.

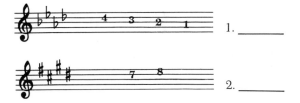

1. A♭

1. _____

2. E

2. _____

Write the major key name for these two key signatures.

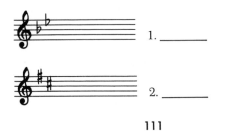

1. B♭

1. _____

2. D

2. _____

111

Write the major key name for these two key signatures.

1. A

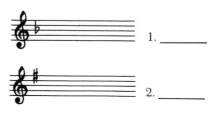

1. _____

2. Eb

2. _____

Write the major key name for these key signatures.

1. F

1. _____

2. G

2. _____

Write the major key name for these two key signatures.

1. Gb

1. _____

2. B

2. _____

A composer wishing to write a song based on the major
scale of C would not have to use any s_____ or
f_____ in his music because in the scale of C the
half steps and whole steps are already located between
steps 3 and 4 and between steps 7 and _____.

sharps

flats

8

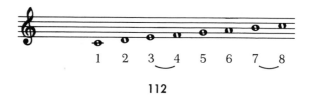

1   2   3   4   5   6   7   8

112

C

If *no* sharps and *no* flats are needed for the key of C major, this must be the key signature for the major key of _____.

C
B

This is the key signature for the major key of _____. The name of the note on the staff is _____.

Write the major key name for these two key signatures.

1. C

2. B♭

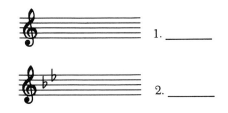

1. _____

2. _____

E♭
G

This is the key signature for the major key of _____. The name of the note on the staff is _____.

You have been given two rules for identifying key signatures. You can apply the rules to figure out that one sharp in a signature will mean that it is the key signature for the major key of G. Or you may just *remember* that a signature with one sharp will *always* be the key signature for the major key of G. Musicians don't use the rules. They merely remember key signatures as you remember the names of certain people. Now, if you forget, for example, that two flats are *always* the key signature for the major key of B♭, you can apply the rule you have learned

No answer
required.

D

D

A

A, C♯

G

F♯

E

F

F

E

and figure it out. If you can merely remember some of these, however, it will speed you tremendously in working with key signatures.

This is the key signature for the major key of _____. Whenever you see *two sharps* in a signature, you can count on the fact that this is the key signature for the major key of _____.

This is the key signature for the major key of _____. This will always be the key signature for the major key of _____. The name of the note on this staff is _____. A suggestion: Always look carefully at the key signature *before* naming the note.

This is the key signature for the major key of _____. The name of the note on the staff is _____.

The name of the note on the staff is _____. This is the key signature for the major key of _____.

This is the key signature for the major key of _____. The name of the note on the staff is _____.

114

Ab
Bb

This is the key signature for the major key of _____.
The name of the note on the staff is _____.

F

F

This is the key signature for the major key of _____.
That means that the name of the first scale step and the
eighth scale step will always be _____.

1   8

D

D
E

This is the key signature for the major key of _____.
The first and eighth scale steps in this key are named
_____. The name of the note on the second step of the
scale in this key is _____.

G

G
C

This is the key signature for the major key of _____.
The first and eighth scale steps in this key are named
_____. The name of the note on the fourth step of the
scale in this key is _____.

Eb

G

This is the key signature for the major key of _____.
The name of the note on the third step of the scale in this
key is _____.

115

Eb

3

This is the key signature for the major key of _____.
This note is scale step number _____ in the scale of this
key.

A

8 or 1

This is the key signature for the major key of _____.
This note is scale step number _____ in the scale of this
key.

D

B

6

This is the key signature for the major key of _____.
The name of the note on the staff is _____. This note
is scale step number _____ in this key.

note, one

beat

The bottom number of a time signature (meter signature)
tells us what kind of a _____ receives _____
_____.

Eb

Bb

5

This is the key signature in the major key of _____.
The name of the note is _____. This note is scale step
number _____ in this key.

Ab

Bb

2

This is the key signature for the major key of _____.
The name of the note on the staff is _____. This note
is scale step number _____ in this key.

116

2
B

This note is scale step number _____ in the major scale of this key. Name this note. _____

6
G

This note is scale step number _____ in the major scale of this key. Name this note. _____

C
B
7

This is the key signature for the major key of _____. The name of this note is _____. This note is scale step number _____ in the major scale of this key.

CHAPTER 7

Relative Minor and Key Signatures

In this chapter you will be introduced to the concept of the relative minor and minor key signatures. You will also learn to locate or identify notes on the scale steps of a minor scale.

If you would like to test your knowledge of this information before reading this chapter, answer the questions below. After completing all of the questions, check your answers with the correct ones on the next page. If you are sure that you are unable to answer these questions, turn the page now.

Criterion Questions

1. This is scale step number _____ in the minor scale of this key.

2. This is scale step number _____ in the minor scale of this key.

3. This is the key signature for the minor key of _____.

4. This is the key signature for the minor key of _____.

Here are the correct answers to the criterion questions on the preceding page:

    1. 5
    2. 3
    3. G
    4. G♯

If you missed an answer, or if you do not feel sure of yourself when answering questions of this kind, turn the page and begin with the first frame.

If you were able to get all four answers correct, you may skip to the beginning of Chapter 8.

scales	You have learned a great deal about *major scales* and *key signatures*. Now we will learn about *minor* _____ and key signatures.
whole	We said that a certain arrangement of half steps and whole steps is necessary in order to have a major scale. Likewise, *minor* scales have their own pattern of half steps and _____ steps.
key	We also said that each major scale and major key has its own *key signature*. We learned that one can usually name the key by looking at the key signature. Similarly, each minor scale has its _____ signature.
related	We say that a brother and a sister are *related*. We say the same thing about major and minor scales and keys. They are also _____.
related	A brother and sister are two entirely different people, but being related, they often share the same house. Certain major and minor scales share the *same key signature* because they are _____.
relative	Every major scale has a *relative minor* scale. Likewise, every major key has a _____ minor key. There are three forms of the minor scale. The minor key signature is derived from the form known as the natural minor.
related	For example, this is the key signature for an F major scale *and also* all forms of the D minor scale. In each case, this key signature arranges the half and whole steps in the proper order. We can say that the scales of F major and D minor are _____. The keys of F major and D minor both have one flat in the _____ signature.
key	

122

key

In order to understand how all of this works, here is the key signature for F *major* and also for D *minor*. Both scales have been written out. The F scale is a *major* scale with whole and half steps in the proper places. This particular D scale can not be a *major* scale because another kind of _____ signature would be necessary in order to arrange it into a major scale.

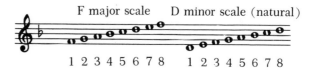

F major scale   D minor scale (natural)

1 2 3 4 5 6 7 8   1 2 3 4 5 6 7 8

1 or 8

6

The note D is scale step number _____ in a D minor scale, but the note D is scale step number _____ in the F major scale.

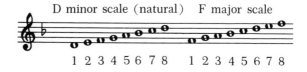

D minor scale (natural)   F major scale

1 2 3 4 5 6 7 8   1 2 3 4 5 6 7 8

Now, here is the way you can usually find the name of the minor key merely by looking at the key signature. In order to find the *minor* key name for a key signature:

1. Find the *major* key name.
2. Find scale step number 6 in the major scale.
3. Scale step number 6 names the minor key for the key signature.

6

minor

Scale step number _____ of the major scale will give you the _____ key name for the key signature.

Let's try to apply this and see how you make out.

1. This is the key signature for the *major* key of

    _____.

G

2. Scale step number 6 in this major scale is named

E

    _____. This names the minor key.

3. Therefore, this is the key signature for the *minor*

E

    key of _____.

Here is another one. This is the key signature for the

A

major key of _____. Scale step number 6 in this major

F♯

scale is named _____. (Watch the sharps!) This is the

A

key signature for the *major* key of _____ and for the

F♯

minor key of _____.

B♭

This is the key signature for the *major* key of _____.

G

Scale step number 6 in this major scale is named _____.

G

This is the key signature for the *minor* scale of _____.

E

This is the key signature for the *major* key of _____.

C♯

This is the key signature for the *minor* key of _____.

C

This is the key signature for the major key of _____.

A

This is the key signature for the minor key of _____.

Ab
F
1

This is the key signature for the *major* key of _____.
This is the key signature for the *minor* key of _____.
This note is scale step number _____ in the *minor* scale
of this key.

Db
Bb
6
1

This is the key signature for the *major* key of _____.
This is the key signature for the *minor* key of _____.
This note is scale step number _____ in the *major*
scale of this key. This note is scale step number _____
in the *minor* scale of this key.

D
B
2
7

This is the key signature for the *major* key of _____.
This is the key signature for the *minor* key of _____.
This note is scale step number _____ in the *minor* scale
of this key. This note is scale step number _____ in
the *major* scale of this key.

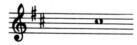

C
A
6
1

This is the key signature for the *major* key of _____.
This is the key signature for the *minor* key of _____.
This note is scale step number _____ in the *major* scale
of this key. This note is scale step number _____ in the
minor scale of this key.

C

This is the key signature for the minor key of _____.

G#

This is the key signature for the minor key of _____.

G

This is the key signature for the *minor* key of _____.

2

This is scale step number _____ in the *minor* scale of this key.

5

This is scale step number _____ in the *minor* scale of this key.

3

This is scale step number _____ in the *minor* scale of this key.

CHAPTER 8

The Natural Sign;
Review of Chapters 1 to 7

The natural sign is introduced at the beginning of this chapter, but most of the chapter is devoted to a review of all that you have learned so far in this book. You should not skip this chapter. It will serve as a check on how well you know the material which has been covered so far and how quickly you can give correct answers to questions of this kind. Work carefully but as rapidly as you can. Begin with the first frame.

F

If a composer places an F sharp in the key signature, this means that all F's in that song are to be played or sung as _____ sharp.

cancels

Now, what happens if he has an F somewhere in that song which he does not want sung or played as F sharp but rather as a plain F, or, as we say it, F natural? All he has to do is place a *natural sign* (♮) in front of that particular F and he will thus *cancel* the effect of the key signature. A natural sign (♮) c_____ the effect of the key signature for any individual note.

C

The note on the staff would usually be sung or played as a C♯ with this key signature. With the natural sign (♮) in front of it, however, the effect of the key signature is now canceled. It is now just a plain _____.

B or B natural

The letter name of this note is _____.

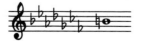

128

The note on the staff could be sounded by striking key number _____ on the keyboard. The letter name of this note is _____.

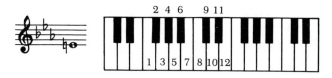

The letter name of this note is _____.

This note is scale step number _____ in the major scale of this key.

Write a note on the staff which is one whole step above the note given. (Look at the keyboard to figure it out if you have to.)

Write a note on the staff which is one half step above the given note.

This is the key signature for the major key of _____.

129

’

F

G

6
A

o

4
*The minor
scale is E.*

The first measure is complete. Draw *one rest* which would accurately complete the second measure. _____

The letter name of this note is _____.

This is the key signature for the *minor* key of _____.

The note on the staff could be sounded by striking key number _____ on the keyboard. The letter name of this note is _____.

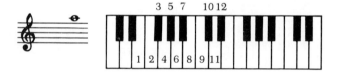

The first measure is complete. Draw *one note* which would accurately complete the second measure. _____

This note is scale step number _____ in the *minor* scale of this key.

130

This note is scale step number _____ in the *major* scale of this key.

Write a note on the staff which is one whole step above the note given.

C

This is the key signature for the major key of _____.

♪

The first measure is complete. Draw *one note* which would complete the second measure. _____

D or D natural

The letter name of this note is _____.

A

This is the key signature for the minor key of _____.

131

Write a note on the staff which is one half step above the note given.

1

The minor scale is C.

This note is scale step number _____ in the minor scale of this key.

3

The major scale is A.

This note is scale step number _____ in the major scale of this key.

Write a note on the staff which is one whole step above the note given. Look carefully at the key signature!

D

This is the key signature for the major key of _____.

Ab

The letter name of this note is _____.

E

This is the key signature for the minor key of _____.

note

one beat

The bottom number of the time signature (meter signature) tells us what kind of a _____ receives _____ _____.

E

The letter name of this note is _____.

Write on the staff a note which is one half step above the given note.

2

The minor scale is F.

This note is scale step number _____ in the minor scale of this key.

4

The major scale is C.

This note is scale step number _____ in the major scale of this key.

beats

measure

The top number of the time signature (meter signature) tells us how many _____ there are in every _____.

Write a note on the staff which is one whole step above the note given.

F

This is the key signature for the major key of _____.

The first measure is complete. Draw *one rest* which would complete the second measure. _____

G or G natural

The letter name of this note is _____.

D

This is the key signature for the minor key of _____.

The first measure is complete. Draw *one rest* which would complete the second measure. _____

3
Eb

The note on the staff could be sounded by striking key number _____ on the keyboard. The letter name of this note is _____. Watch the clef!

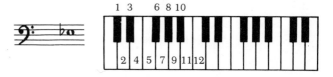

Write a note on the staff which is one half step above the note given.

3
The minor scale is A.

This note is scale step number _____ in the minor scale of this key.

1
The major scale is Db.

This note is scale step number _____ in the major scale of this key.

G

This is the key signature for the major key of _____.

♩

The first measure is complete. Draw *one note* which would complete the second measure. _____

135

C#

The letter name of this note is _____.

C

This is the key signature for the minor key of _____.

♪

The first measure is complete. Draw *one note* which would accurately complete the second measure. _____

5
The minor scale is G.

This note is scale step number _____ in the minor scale of this key.

5
The major scale is F♯.

This note is scale step number _____ in the major scale of this key.

Write on the staff a note which is one whole step above the note given. You had better think about this one!

G♭

This is the key signature for the major key of _____.

136

This note is scale step number _____ in the minor scale of this key.

This is the key signature for the minor key of _____.

The note on the staff could be sounded by striking key number _____ on the keyboard. What is the letter name of this note? _____

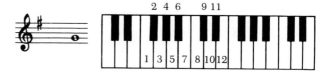

Write a note on the staff which is one half step above the note given.

The first measure is complete. Draw *one note* which would accurately complete the second measure. _____

The letter name of this note is _____.

137

The Sol-Fa
Syllables

In Chapter 9 you will be introduced to one more way of referring to notes. When you have completed this chapter you will be able to name any note by its correct syllable name whether or not it has been altered by a sharp or flat.

If you wish to check your knowledge of this information before beginning this chapter, answer the following question. When you have answered all parts of the question, check your answers on the next page.

Criterion Question

Write, in the appropriate space under each note, the correct syllable name for the note.

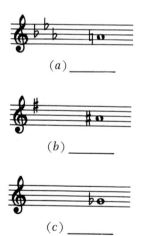

(a) _____

(b) _____

(c) _____

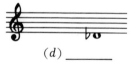

(d) _____

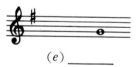

(e) _____

(f) _____

Here are the correct answers to the criterion question on the preceding page:

(*a*) fi   (*d*) ra

(*b*) ri   (*e*) do

(*c*) se   (*f*) fa

If you were able to get all six of the answers correct, you may skip to Chapter 10. If you missed one, begin with the first frame.

So far, we have used numbers and letter names in referring to notes on the staff. In addition to numbers and letters, we sometimes use *syllables*. These are known as the sol-fa syllables. In the sol-fa system, _____ are used to refer to notes on the staff.

syllables

The basic syllables used in this system are do, re mi, fa. sol, la, ti, do. You have, no doubt, heard these names before. (If, by any chance you have not, look at them very carefully and say them without looking at this page.) To be sure you have the correct spelling, write the eight syllables here: _____, _____, _____, _____, _____, _____, _____, _____. These are pronounced doe, ray, mee, fah, so or sole, lah, tee, doe.

do, re, mi, fa
sol, la, ti, do

These eight syllables correspond with the eight scale steps in any key:

do   re   mi   fa   sol   la   ti   do
1   2   3   4   5   6   7   8

To find the syllable name, we always use the major scale, *never* the minor. The note on the staff is scale step number 1 in the major scale of G. The syllable name for this note would be _____. (Look at number 1, above.)

do

Remember that we always use the *major* scale to determine a syllable name, *never* the minor. The note on the staff is scale step number _____ in the major scale of this key. The syllable name for this note would be _____.

1
do

do   re   mi   fa   sol   la   ti   do
1   2   3   4   5   6   7   8

1	The note on the staff is scale step number _____ in the major scale of this key. What is the syllable name?
do	_____

	do	re	mi	fa	sol	la	ti	do
	1	2	3	4	5	6	7	8

Write the syllable names for the three notes on the staff.

_____, _____, _____

do, re, mi	do	re	mi	fa	sol	la	ti	do
The three notes are steps 1, 2, and 3 in the F major scale.	1	2	3	4	5	6	7	8

Write the syllable names for the three notes on the staff.

_____, _____, _____

do, mi, sol	do	re	mi	fa	sol	la	ti	do
These notes are steps 1, 3, and 5 in the D major scale.	1	2	3	4	5	6	7	8

Write the syllable names for the three notes on the staff.

_____, _____, _____

re, sol, la	do	re	mi	fa	sol	la	ti	do
The three notes are scale steps 2, 5, and 6 in the A major scale.								

Write the syllable names for the three notes on the staff.

_____, _____, _____ (Look at the preceding frame for the syllable names if you cannot answer this question.)

la, ti, do
The three notes are scale steps 6, 7, and 8 in the major scale of E♭.

143

fa
mi, la
These notes are
scale steps 4,
3, and 6 in the
major scale of
A♭.

The syllable names for these notes are _____ and _____ and _____.

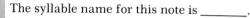

sol
The note is scale
step number 5
in the major
scale of D.

The syllable name for this note is _____.

ti
The note is the
seventh step in
the major
scale of E♭.

The syllable name for this note is _____.

fa
The note is scale
step number 4
in the major
scale of F.

The syllable name for this note is _____.

la
The note is the
sixth step in
the major scale
of C.

The syllable name for this note is _____.

re
The note is step
2 in the key
of B♭.

The syllable name for this note is _____.

144

mi
*The note is step
3 in the key
of G.*

What is the syllable name for this note? _____

do
*The note is step
number 1 in the
key of A.*

The syllable name for this note is _____.

do

half

The G on the staff is step 1 in this scale, so its syllable name is _____. We cannot call the G♯ by the syllable name *do* because the sharp has raised this note one h_____ step higher than do.

When the note for any syllable is raised one half step, we spell the syllable in such a way that it ends in the letter i. The first note on this staff we call *do,* but the second note (the G♯) we call *di,* because it is a *do* which has been raised one half step. Write the syllable names for these two notes:

do, di

— —

do

di

The syllable name for the C on this staff would be _____ because it is step number 1 in this scale. The syllable name for the C♯ would be _____ because it is a *do* which has been *raised* one half step. (Remember that when any syllable is raised a half step, you change the spelling so it ends with the letter i.)

145

do
di

The syllable name for the D on the staff is _____. The syllable name for the D♯ is _____ because it is a *do* which has been raised one half step by the sharp.

The syllable name for the A on the staff is do. The syllable name for the A♯ is _____.

di

Whenever a *sharp* or a *flat* or a *natural sign* appears before a note, you will probably have to alter the syllable name. If there is *no* sharp, flat, or natural sign before a note, you _____ [will/will not] have to alter the syllable name.

will not

For example, the *first* note on the staff is a C, which is the fourth step in this major key of G. We would call this note by the syllable name _____. Now the second note has been altered with a sharp, so we _____ [can/cannot] call this note fa.

fa

cannot

The *first* note we call *fa*. The second note is a fa which has been *raised* one half step by the sharp, so we call this note *fi*. The syllable name for the first note is _____ and the syllable name for the second note is _____.

fa

fi

146

la

li

The first note on the staff is the sixth step in the scale, so we give it the syllable name _____. The second note is a la which has been raised one half step, so we give it the syllable name _____. (Remember that when the note is raised, the syllable name ends in i.)

do

di

The syllable name for the first note is _____ .
The syllable name for the second note is _____.

re

ri

The syllable name for the first note on the staff is _____.
The syllable name for the second note on the staff is _____. (It ends in i.)

do

di

If this note had *no* sharp in front of it, we would call it _____. With the sharp in front of it, however, we must call it _____.

fi

The syllable name for this note is _____.

sol

If there were no sharp in front of this note we would call it _____. With the sharp we call it *si*.

sol, si

If there were no sharp in front of this note, we would call it _____. With the sharp we call it _____.

si

The syllable name for this note is _____.

re, ri

If this note had no sharp in front of it, we would call it _____. With the sharp, however, we must call it _____.

li

The syllable name for this note is _____.

si

The syllable name for this note is _____.

do, fi

Write the syllable names for these notes. _____, _____

148

ri

The syllable name for this note is _____.

What are the syllable names for these three notes?
_____, _____, _____

mi, ti, si

la
li

Write the syllable names for these two notes. _____,
_____

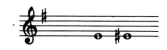

Write the syllable names for the three notes on the staff.
_____, _____, _____

do, di, re

fa
sol

Write the syllable names for these two notes. _____,
_____

A flat in front of a note lowers the note by one half
step. A sharp placed in front of a note will _____
[lower/raise] the note by one half step.

raise

A *natural sign* (♮) cancels the effect of a f_____
or a sharp.

flat

149

Without the *natural sign* (♮) this note would be A♭. With the natural in front of it, however, it is no longer an A♭ but just a plain _____.

A

This note has been lowered by the flat in the key signature. It is now B♭. If a natural sign were placed in front of the note it would _____ [raise/lower] the note back to B again.

raise

This note has been raised one half step by the sharp in the key signature. It is now F♯. If a natural sign were placed in front of the note, it would _____ [raise/lower] the note back to F again.

lower

You can now see that if a natural sign is placed in front of a note, it will *lower* the note when there are *sharps* in the key signature and it will _____ [raise/lower] the note when there are *flats* in the key signature.

raise

raised

It would be A♭
with this key
signature, but
the natural
sign cancels
the flat and
raises it to A.
See A♭ to A
on the
keyboard.

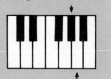

raise

re

raised

(from E♭ to E)

lower

The natural sign (♮) in front of the note has _____ [raised/lowered] this note by one half step.

A natural sign in front of a note will _____ [raise/lower] the note when there are *flats* in the key signature.

The syllable name for this note is _____.

The natural sign in front of this note has _____ [raised/lowered] the note by one half step.

A natural sign in front of a note will _____ [raise/lower] the note when there are *sharps* in the key signature.

151

lowered

(from C♯ to C)

la

raised

(from B♭ to B)

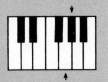

lowered

(from G♯ to G)

fa

This note, A♭, is the fourth scale step in the key of E♭.

fi

The natural sign in front of this note has _____ [raised/lowered] the note by one half step.

The syllable name for this note is _____.

The natural sign in front of this note has _____ [raised/lowered] the note by one half step.

The natural sign in front of this note has _____ [raised/lowered] the note by one half step.

The syllable name for this note is _____.

Here is the same note (fa) except that the natural sign has raised it one half step. A *fa* which has been *raised* one half step is called _____.

fa, raises
fi

Without the natural sign, the syllable name for this note would be _____. But the natural sign _____ [raises/lowers] it one half step, so it is called _____.

sol

What is the syllable name for this note? _____

si

The syllable name for this note is _____.

re

The syllable name for this note is _____.

ri

The syllable name for this note is _____.

di

If we find that a certain syllable has been raised one half step, we change the spelling of the syllable so that it ends in the letter i. If *do* is raised a half step, it becomes _____.

ri

If *re* is raised one half step, it becomes _____. You will never find *mi* or *ti* raised, so you don't have to worry about them at all. If *fa* is raised a half step it becomes

fi

_____.

153

If *sol* is raised one half step, it becomes _____. If *la* is raised a half step, it becomes _____.

Now what happens when a syllable is *lowered* one half step? All you do is change the spelling so that it ends in the letter e. The note on the staff would usually be called *la* but it has been *lowered* one half step by the flat, so we would call it _____. (Make it end with the letter e.)

Without the flat in front of it, this note would be called _____. The flat lowers it a half step, however, so we call it _____.

Without the flat, the syllable name for this note would be _____. With the flat, however, the syllable name for this note would have to be _____. (It must end with an e.)

Without the flat, the syllable name for this note would be _____. With the flat, the syllable name is _____.

If this note had no flat in front of it, we would call it *sol*. If it had a *sharp* in front of it, we would call it *si*. With a

se

flat in front of it, however, we must call it _____. (Make it end with an e.)

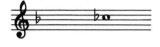

When a syllable is lowered one half step, there is one exception about ending the syllable with the letter e. It occurs with the syllable *re*. This, of course, already ends in e so when it is lowered, it becomes *ra*. The note on the staff would be called _____.

ra

re
*F♯ is scale step
number 2 in
this key.*

The syllable name for this note is _____.

ra
*The note was
lowered from
F♯ to F.*

The syllable name for this note is _____.

le
*The note was
lowered from
C♯ to C.*

The syllable name for this note is _____.

sol

The syllable name for this note is _____.

155

se

The syllable name for this note is _____.

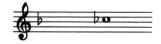

ra

The syllable name for this note is _____.

te

The syllable name for this note is _____.

me

The syllable name for this note is _____.

ra

The syllable name for this note is _____.

In working with syllables we should remember that if we find that a certain syllable has been *raised* (by either a natural or a sharp) we change the spelling of the syllable so that it ends in the letter _____.

i

If we find a syllable which has been *lowered* (by a natural sign or a flat) we change the spelling so that it ends with the letter _____. The one *exception* to this is the syllable *re* which becomes _____ when it is lowered.

e
ra

Watch for the flats, sharps, or natural signs which appear *immediately* in front of certain notes. This is your clue that the syllable name for that note will probably be altered. *Nothing* appears *immediately* in front of this note (we are not counting the key signature), so we know that its syllable name will be one of the basic syllables (do, re, mi, fa, sol, la, _____, do).

ti

Here, this note has been altered by a sign *immediately* in front of the note. The syllable name for this note will probably be one of the _____ [basic/altered] syllable names.

altered

Write the syllable names for these two notes. _____ _____

sol
te

The syllable names for these two notes are _____ and _____.

mi
si

If we find a note which has been *raised* (by means of a sharp or a natural sign) we change the spelling of the syllable so that it ends with the letter _____.

i

What are the syllable names for these two notes? _____ _____

re
si

157

ti

The syllable name for this note is _____.

do
fa, me

Write the syllable names for these three notes. _____
_____ _____

la
le

What are the syllable names for these two notes? _____
_____

mi
di, re

Give the syllable names for these three notes. _____,
_____, _____

e

If we find a note which has been *lowered* (by means of a flat or a natural sign) we adjust the spelling of the syllable so that it ends with the letter _____. The one *exception* to this rule comes with the syllable *re* which

ra

becomes _____ when it is lowered a half step.

se
ra

The syllable names for these two notes are _____ and
_____.

158

fi

The syllable name for this note is _____.

ri

The syllable name for this note is _____.

CHAPTER 10

Summary

This chapter will provide you with a complete summary and review of all that has been taught in this book. Answer each question carefully and you will find out exactly how well you know the material. Do this chapter as rapidly as you can without making careless mistakes.

If you find that you are missing one particular kind of question each time it appears, you may wish to refer to the chapter which deals with that question in order to refresh your memory.

Good luck on this chapter. See if you can do it quickly and at the same time make it 100 per cent correct.

Write on the staff a note which is one whole step above the given note.

Write the syllable name for this note in the major scale of this key. _____

se

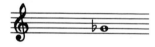

Write on the staff a note which is one whole step above the given note.

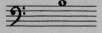
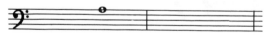

In the major scale of this key, this note is scale step number _____.

3

The first measure is complete. Draw *one rest* which would complete the second measure. _____

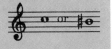

Write on the staff a note which is one half step above the given note.

The first measure is complete. Draw *one rest* which would complete the second measure. _____

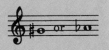

Write on the staff a note which is one half step above the given note.

2

In the minor scale of this key, this note is scale step number _____.

The first measure is complete. Draw *one rest* which would complete the second measure. _____

5

o

A

5

1

ti

In the minor scale of this key, this note is scale step number _____.

The first measure is complete. Draw one note which would complete the second measure. _____

The letter name for this note is _____.

In the major scale of this key, this note is scale step number _____.

In the major scale of this key, this note is scale step number _____.

Write the syllable name for this note in the major scale of this key. _____

F#

This is the key signature for the major key of _____.

do

Write the syllable name for this note in the major scale of this key. _____

6

In the major scale of this key, this note is scale step number _____.

B

This is the key signature for the minor key of _____.

Write on the staff a note which is one whole step above the given note.

D#

The letter name for this note is _____.

3

In the minor scale of this key, this note is scale step number _____.

165

C or C natural

The letter name for this note is _____.

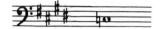

C

This is the key signature for the major key of _____.

♩

The first measure is complete. Draw one note which would complete the second measure. _____

𝄾

The first measure is complete. Draw *one rest* which would complete the second measure. _____

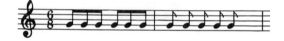

di

Write the syllable name for this note in the major scale of this key. _____

ra

Write the syllable name for this note in the major scale of this key. _____

E

The letter name for this note is _____.

Write on the staff a note which is one half step above the given note.

re

Write the syllable name for this note in the major scale of this key. _____

F♯

This is the key signature for the minor key of _____.

The first measure is complete. Draw one note which would complete the second measure. _____

B♭

This is the key signature for the minor key of _____.

4

In the minor scale of this key, this note is scale step number _____.

—

The first measure is complete. Draw *one rest* which would complete the second measure. _____

E♭

This is the key signature for the minor key of _____.

fa

Write the syllable name for this note in the major scale of this key. _____

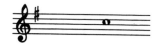

re

Write the syllable name for this note in the major scale of this key. _____

si

Write the syllable name for this note in the major scale of this key. _____

fi

Write the syllable name for this note in the major scale of this key. _____

Write on the staff a note which is one whole step above the given note.

C♯

This is the key signature for the major key of _____.

C

The letter name for this note is _____.

A

This is the key signature for the minor key of _____.

Write on the staff a note which is one half step above the given note.

Write on the staff a note which is one half step above the given note.

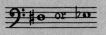

1

In the minor scale of this key, this note is scale step number _____.

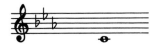

169

la

Write the syllable name for this note in the major scale of this key. _____

mi

Write the syllable name for this note in the major scale of this key. _____

♩

The first measure is complete. Draw one note which would complete the second measure. _____

2

In the minor scale of this key, this note is scale step number _____.

F

This is the key signature for the minor key of _____.

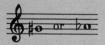

Write on the staff a note which is one whole step above the given note.

G♯

This is the key signature for the minor key of _____.

170

3

le

D♭

mi

4

Write on the staff a note which is one half step above the given note.

In the major scale of this key, this note is scale step number _____.

Write the syllable name for this note in the major scale of this key. _____

This is the key signature for the major key of _____.

Write the syllable name for this note in the major scale of this key. _____

In the major scale of this key, this note is scale step number _____.